# THE FISH HORN ALARM

## More Stories of Country Folk Life

by

J. Sheldon Fisher

*Author of The Groaning Tree*

Empire State Books
Interlaken, New York
1994

First Printing — June 1994

Manufactured in the United States of America
Library of Congress Catalogue Number 94–71617
ISBN: 1–55787–025–X

A *quality* publication of
Heart of the Lakes Publishing
Interlaken, New York 14847

# Contents

# *The Fish Horn Alarm*

When the Fishers telephone exchange office was moved from the corner of Fowler and Railroad Streets, that building became the home of Mary Esther Hill. She was the daughter of Jerome Hill, who lived at the southern end of Wangum Road and was involved in the infamous schoolhouse tug-of-war. Her brother, Homer Jerome Hill, was the noted horse racer who owned a fine stable at the intersection of Lower Fishers and Log Cabin Roads. A sister by the name of "Vina" or "Vine" married a local Civil War veteran by the name of Hiram French. They pioneered in the Dakota Territory at a place called LeMoure. He died there about 1893.

Mary Esther Hill went by the name of "Ett." I do not recall much about Ett before 1913 other than that she was one of the many neighbors who walked to the Post Office after the frequent mail trains.

What made her distinctive in the community over the years was the fact that she was afraid of dying without any person knowing about it, so she bought two tin fish horns. One she kept by her bed and the other she carried in a specially made quiver suspended by a strap slung over her shoulder. She took this with her whenever she left the house. The idea of the fish horn was that it was easy to blow and the sound was loud and raucus. Ett made it well known that when she blew that horn, it meant that she felt that she was about to die and wanted help.

Ett kept her kitchen well stocked with food from her fine

The house on Fowler Street in Fishers where Ett Hill blew the "Fish Horn." Her sister stands on the porch.

garden and with home canned goods. She tramped the fields and woods gathering fruits and wild berries, from which she made the finest jams and jellies. Often the woods and the valley would echo with the blasts of the fish horn when she was overly fatigued and thought that she would die before she got home. Any farmer or passerby would usually go to her rescue. She would even blow the fish horn if she hurried too much and got out of breath going to one of the grocery stores or to the Post Office. She found that it was a good attention-getter when there was nothing else to do, because a blast or two would always bring some person to provide the conversation which she loved.

For years it was a trying situation for the neighbor women on Fowler Street who were expected to rush to Ett's aid when the fish horn blew. It was an absolute certainty that if there was an electric storm, either night or day, the fish horn would blow. Many were the nights that our family would be awakened by that blasted fish horn heard across town. The women who bore the brunt of the night calls were Melissa Hunt Smith, Helen Barry, and Mrs. Jack "Fiddler" Barry, and Cecelia Smith, who lived on the East Main Street hill and was also awakened. The old fable about crying wolf too often never bothered the neighbors—in their kindness they always went to her house in case it was an emergency.

One day an unusual thing happened in town. A red-paneled Ford Model T truck drove around through the streets with a fish horn blowing. Some person got on the phone and called others saying that Ett Hill was driving a truck and thinks that she will die if she can't stop it. We soon learned that it was a man selling fish. For several years the fish man came around on a regular schedule, so we soon learned which person was blowing the fish horn. When Ett Hill later broke her leg the fish horn did come in handy to call for help.

Vine French eventually came back from LaMoure to take care of her sister. I remember Mrs. French as a very stately-looking woman on her visits to Fishers. On her last visit, when Ett's leg bone had healed, every effort was made to get her to walk, but she refused to do anything for herself. On February 24, 1928, when Ett Hill was actually dying, she could not summon the strength to blow the horn. When her things were sold at auction, I bought her two fish horns, not to use myself, but to save as interesting artifacts of local history.

# Old Hazards of
# Trolley Riding

When the interurban trolleys were new, they were hailed as a great boon to the development of the countryside. They would bring many city dwellers to the country to live. Instead, they worked in reverse. They made it easier for country youth to escape from hard farm life to less strenuous employment in the city.

When the Rochester and Eastern Rapid Railway from Geneva to Rochester was completed on June 15, 1904, the terminal, for a time, was at Main Street, Fishers. The cars went both ways every hour; specials, which included milk and freight cars, were in between.

Near Wood's Stop on the Lower Fishers Road, the Adams Farm was laid out as a large subdivision for Rochesterians mad rush to "The Beautiful Land of Fishers." Nothing happened, for the city dwellers had no need to leave. However, nature lovers did come on weekends and got off at Sullivan's Stop, a quarter of a mile west at Log Cabin Road.

A person's first ride on the trolley was often a frightening experience. The huge car sped over 60 miles an hour up and down high hills and around sharp curves. I have seen hunting dogs riding in the back vestibule getting nauseated. It was as bad as riding the Sea Breeze Jack-Rabbit Roller Coaster.

Being a one-track road with cars going both ways, with no control system, the hazards of human error were very great. The problem was mitigated when a signal system was installed on

November 1, 1913.

The trolley cars were usually overcrowded coming out of the city after work. I always got on last in order to give the older people a chance at a seat. On one occasion, I was hanging on the second step until the car picked up to top speed. I had just reached the vestibule when the unexpected happened. The first and second steps were torn off when the trolley hit a loose plank protruding beside the rail.

* * *

The Crossman's Pond Stop on Benson Road had a siding switch in order to allow trolleys to pass. A motorman had a fancied grudge against jolly Conductor "Hank" Gardner. When the motorman found that it was Gardner's trolley for which he had to take the siding, he yelled, "I will get you for this." After a short lapse of time opening and closing the switch and placing the kite on the main cable, he raced after Gardner's trolley.

Conductor Gardner discharged passengers at Wood's and had started up the grade when the mad motorman crashed into the rear end of Gardner's trolley. The crash broke five of Gardner's ribs, injured passengers, and killed a man. Fred Connelly of Fishers had his arm broken. Leon Aldrich carted the injured next door to the farmhouse of Orrin Adams; they were shortly removed by another trolley to the Canandaigua Hospital. Leon Aldrich of Valentown Road was there in his cutter on that snowy day in November, 1912 to pick up Lloyd Benson and his aunt. Leon had described the event to me.

* * *

On the morning of August 1, 1913 the kite pulley broke off while on the wide curve around Crossman's Pond. My good friend Conductor George Ottley of Canandaigua and Motorman

Ed Dwyer of Pittsford were in charge of the Orange Limited headed toward Geneva. The trolley wouldn't run unless the kite pole was touching the power cable. By leaning out of the back window Conductor Ottley could keep the pole touching the cable by guiding the rope. As the trolley roared around the curve, Ottley lost his balance and fell out the back window onto the stone ballast. After coasting for a half mile without power, others helped in backing up, where they found George Ottley unconscious. They rushed him to the Canandaigua Hospital, where they found a number of broken bones and many bruises.

The kite on a trolley is a long pole with a pulley wheel running along the power cable. Our trolley was going along smoothly when the kite bounced off and the metal pole hit the cable. Like a bolt of lightening it came down through the roof, breaking glass all around me and setting fire to the water closet at my back. No one was injured but we were all quite surprised. The same thing happened another time at the Fishers Station siding when the trolley kite went down on the siding cable, shorted and burned part of the roof off car 157.

* * *

Another serious accident took place at Wood's Stop just four months before safety signals were installed. On Saturday afternoon, July 13, 1913, an excursion express was heading for Canandaigua to meet a boat. A freight trolley had orders to take the siding at Fishers in order to let the express car pass by. It did not do so, and they crashed head-on just before Wood's Stop.

Because of this failure, Edward S. Ward of the Ward Natural Science Museum in Rochester was killed, and eighteen others were seriously injured. One of several expected to die was 23-year old Harry Ament, but he did not. He was a frequent visitor at our house years later. Four doctors cared for the injured at the home of Orrin Adams. The injured were taken by special car to the hospital in Canandaigua. The two totally-wrecked trolleys, firmly locked together, were towed to the Fishers siding. The roofs of both cars were torn off. The seats were torn out half the length of the passenger car. The newspaper stories mentioned that the freight car was the same car that had collided with a work train at Fishers the previous year

* * *

The final trolley ran to Rochester on the night of July 31, 1930. The conductor was Charles J. Browne of Canandaigua, who gathered up the change carrier, fire extinguisher, unused tickets, his conductor's hat and later gave them all to me. The Motorman, Ed Dwyer, gave me his hat with the silver plated badge and his original large photo of the world-famous trolley train race between Victor and Fishers, which proved that the electric trolley was faster than the steam train.

# *Train Watchers*

Train watching was a very important pastime for some of the residents of Fishers. It had been so since the first train went through on September 10, 1840. One never knew when a new type of locomotive would be pulling a train, breathing hard and hissing steam pulsations as if it were a live creature. Therefore, not to miss any good sightings, all trains had to be watched.

It was a great thrill when the world famous 999 locomotive, which had made the first 100 mile an hour run in 1893, was, years later, rerouted through Fishers.

For a long period, passenger locomotives had a high smoke stack and high drive wheels while freight locomotives had smaller wheels with the frame and boiler built for power and not speed. Each engine was numbered and many watchers kept a record until all were seen and recorded.

When there was track trouble between Rochester and Lyons, the great passenger trains like the 20th Century Limited and the Empire State Express were rerouted over the Auburn Road via Fishers to Geneva and then to Lyons back on the Main Line and it was especially exciting when a complete Pennsylvania Railroad passenger train came from Philadelphia up their line to Canandaigua and on to Rochester as a special. Their Pullman coaches were a maroon color and were pleasing to watch contrasted to the dull black of the Auburn Road cars.

The crowning achievement for all train watchers to see was the one of a kind, well-polished and trimly-built Pony Engine

Auburn Road train on the New York Central on the mile stretch
between Fishers and Railroad Mills

on its annual run. It had a high drive wheel with the observation cabs built on the side of the boiler. This picturesque locomotive was for the special use of top railroad officials on their tours of inspection. The whistle had a high pitch and the running sound was a sharp staccato burst of steam and smoke. No one wanted to miss it. The desire seemed so great that it made the adrenaline flow faster when it was seen.

Therefore, it was not strange when one of the Fishers train watchers was on his deathbed he heard the magic Pony Engine, and an unusual thing happened. He revived enough to look out the window to see his cherished locomotive, and he lived to see it for several more years.

Abandoned home of the notorious Morrisey Gang, located at the corner of Mile Square Road and Main Street, Fishers. The cistern was kept filled with hard cider instead of rainwater. It was burned by the Mendon Fire Department in July, 1950.

# Poverty Huddle and Hobo Hell

At the end of Main Street, Fishers, at Mile Square Road was one of the roughest and toughest places known in New York State. This isolated place just one mile west of the very active railroad station and Fishers Post Office was over the Ontario-Monroe County line in the Town of Mendon.

It was a private prison farm operated by the Morrisey Gang, a ruthless bunch of men who captured unsuspecting hobos by getting them drunk. When they became somewhat sober the next morning, they were taken out to the fields and forced to do farm work. If the hobo objected, he was beaten until he begged to work. For those who escaped, it was no job to replace them as it was easy to capture others.

It was known as Poverty Huddle because of the Irish immigrant shacks on this farm prior to the Civil War. One of the later arrivals was John Morris, who it is said married a husky Indian woman. Through hard work they prospered, purchased the huddle and added more acres up the hill to Poverty Pinch on the Mendon Road. Because of his financial success, he proclaimed himself, "King of the Huddle," and built up a court of followers who provided for his every whim. He assumed the name of Morrisey to imitate some ancient Irish nobleman he was always talking about. Instead of working on the railroad, or being a policeman, or going into politics, as did many of his countrymen, he was content with collecting fine horses and raising beef cattle. This provided a good income.

Into this setting were born two sons, Thomas and John. "Old Tom," as he was later called, was a giant of a man who must have weighed around 350 pounds. I will never forget his hands, for they were twice the size of any other man's I have ever met. His younger brother, John or Jack, was like a tall beanpole. It looked comical when the two brothers were together. Jack was tough-looking, but was not a very good fighter and always kept close to his brother Tom, when there was trouble. This gave him the nickname of "Shadow." He had a dirty stubble of a beard and was always madly chewing tobacco when not drinking. The brothers were heavy drinkers, but had a great tolerance of the affects of alcohol. I never saw them drunk.

Old Tom had the most complete collection of oaths and curses that any one person could possibly accumulate and use. Every third word was punctuated with an oath. A mild one was "Goddam it to hell." Strange to say, no one seemed to take offense at his language.

Downtown Rochester was only fourteen miles away. Front Street was on the west side of the Genesee River with its notorious flop houses and saloons. Here in a Bowery-like fashion gathered the hobos and roustabouts from the railroad yards, the source of the Morriseys' shanghaied laborers. Old Tom was a favorite person of the saloon keepers and restaurant operators, for the amount of business which he gave them, and of a taxi company which hauled his victims to the last trolley car out of the city.

When there was a prison break at the Huddle, new bums had to be captured. Several strong-armed men, along with Old Tom, would drive a team of horses with a lumber wagon to the Fishers trolley station and tie the horses to the old apple tree until they came back at night. My sisters, Ella, Helen and Mary, often got off the trolley after a day at school and drove the team the one mile to our house and then let the horses find their way home. This meant that a special trip by a guard had to be made back to the station to meet the 12:30 night owl trolley to haul the drunken human captives to the Huddle.

Old Tom would spend part of his day buying horses on the public market to be delivered to his farm while his men scouted for able-bodied men. Old Tom then posed as a wealthy farmer who was interested in sharing his prosperity with the less fortunate traveler. The weary "men of the road" welcomed a much needed rest and vacation at "the country estate." I heard the sales pitch many times and the midnight tales of all of the land which he owned, as his wagons passed our house.

When the men arrived, they were stripped of their possessions and locked in rooms until morning. They were given a good breakfast and taken to the fields to work. At noon the men were given a meal with sufficient hard cider to keep them docile. At night to keep them quiet until morning, more cider was given them. Clean clothes and washed dishes were unknown. The kitchen sink pump was not for water but for hard cider as the cistern in the cellar held sixty barrels. I know, because I once helped to fill it from the Fishers cider mill.

The appearance of the house, barn and yard was unimaginable. Chickens, horses, sheep, cows, and filth were all blended together. Tough-looking characters were all around. A huge straw stack was off to one side between the house and barns, so when animals were fed they scattered straw and hay all over. At threshing time I helped farmers on the steam threshing rigs, but always avoided the Morrisey job.

Along with farming, Old Tom's main business was horse

trading. He always got extra value to boot and very, very few traders could say that they bested him in a deal. However, there was one horse trade Old Tom thought that he had won but didn't. Mr. Austin from Pittsford told me he got a magnificent looking horse in trade from Old Tom. He was driving it home and as he was crossing the Cartersville canal bridge on East Street, the reins accidently got under the horse's tail. The horse screamed and kicked the buggy to bits and then began attacking Mr. Austin in a frenzied rage. Nearby workmen had to kill the horse in order to save Mr. Austin. Old Tom was forced to make good on the deal, since he did not reveal that the animal was very dangerous and goosey.

I got to know Old Tom and his "shadow" because they rented part of our farm. I watched the shanghaied men help do the plowing and dragging the fields under the watchful eyes of the guards. When I carried drinking water to them, they would tell me of the beatings and tortures the men would get if they didn't obey orders promptly. They all schemed to escape.

Although the Morriseys never paid any wages, they did provide plenty of food and hard cider. I used to watch as they bought a wagon load of groceries at Fowler's store. It meant that no one else could get waited on until the Morriseys left.

Several women were in residence at the Morrisey domicle headed by burly Annie, the main cook. Many bloody fights took place among the gang to decide whose turn it was to sleep with Annie. One night Annie got off the seven-thirty train, well fortified with alcohol, and came to our house. She wanted my mother to have me light her way home with a lantern. She promised to take good care of me away from the hobos and would let me sleep with her, then I could come back in the morning with the lantern. The first thing that I thought of was the filth and vermin. My mother thanked her for her neighborly offer and suggested that she bring the lantern back at her convenience, which she did. I was eleven at the time.

Like an old horse trader, Old Tom never made a bet unless he felt absolutely sure that he would win. In a weak moment at the Fishers Hotel bar, after hearing Charles Evans Hughes speak at the station in his campaign for the presidency against Woodrow Wilson, Old Tom bet on Hughes. The loser was to drink a gallon of kerosene and eat a cake of soap. The payoff took place in front of Fowler's store, where Old Tom got his first introduction to a cake of soap, which he ate, and then drank a gallon of kerosene because Wilson won. I should add that kerosene was so refined then that it was not as poisonous as it is today.

If any person or group did any harm or insulted any member of the gang, it was a serious offense and called for punishment. Once an individual made a slurring remark to one of the Morrisey guards. A force of fifteen men left the Huddle to seek out the offender, who was on a work-bee on Phillips Road near the Lehigh Valley's Fisherville station. At Fishers there were fifteen men in this work-bee who didn't expect a fight. It was a violent fight that was talked about for years. Clubs, pitchforks, stones, knives and bare knuckles were used. No one was killed in this bloody event, although men were lying all over the fields and roads. Those of the Morrisey gang who were able to run were chased all of the way home. This was described to me years ago by my cousin, Charlie Fisher.

One time Old Tom got into a fight with Ernest Barry which lasted for eight hours and even disrupted rail traffic at the Fishers station. Why it started no one can recall. Never before had anyone seen such slugging, even by professional boxers. Barry was about a third the size of Morrisey, but very fast on his feet. Seemingly he was no match for Old Tom. Word got around at Bushnell's Basin, Mendon and Victor about the fight, and many came. The hotel customers made bets on the fight and the saloon did a thriving business. A hunter with a high powered rifle, who had placed a bet at the bar, slammed his gun down so hard that it discharged through the ceiling and out the roof. Without drawing blood, the bullet passed between the arm and body of a man sleeping in the bedroom above. Today the bullet hole is marked for the curious to see. Neither fighter was knocked out. Towards sunset the fight was stopped and called a draw with all bets returned.

Another fight, which I well remember, happened about the spring of 1915. It all came about when the third blacksmith shop was opened in town by a man named William DeGraw. The blacksmith was a short, wiry man of good strength and was supposed to have been a professional boxer. The local agitators saw a good chance to stir up a fight. One person went to Bill and told him that Tom Morrisey resented his opening another shop in Fishers without his permission, and he was going to drive him out. Another fellow went to Old Tom and told him that the new blacksmith was telling around that Old Tom was a murderer, a no-good drunk and a cheat, the two could not live in the same town together and that he would drive Old Tom out on sight.

The day arrived when Old Tom drove up in his one-horse open buggy and entered the hotel. Bill DeGraw was hurried over and the two met. Such an exhibition of ferocity the agitators never expected to see. Some of the visitors didn't get a chance to escape and were trampled upon. DeGraw was thrown upon the pool table and then he jumped down on Old Tom. They rolled and fought on the floor, behind the bar, and into the kitchen. Bill ran out the front door as the stove was thrown at him. No one seems to remember for sure who the winner really was, but actually the loser was Jim O'Brien, whose place was left a shambles. It was fun watching it from a distance.

However, the frightful conditions of the Morrisey forced labor farm continued on as usual. Men escaped and men were known to have died. The law either didn't seem to care, because they were unwanted bums, or were afraid to do anything about it. When the New York State Police was organized in 1917, they made a few visits here on horseback but only dared to come in groups of two or four men. When George Van Voorhis, who lived on the next road, was sheriff of Ontario County, he more or less let the gang fight it out among themselves. Old Tom never resisted arrest, and no charge ever stuck.

A good example was the death of a huge hulk of a man Old Tom captured on one of his raids on the Front Street saloons in Rochester. The morning after this captive became sober enough to be taken with the others out to the fields for work, but he strongly objected. He was about equal in strength to Old Tom. The struggle became violent to the point that the hobo grabbed an ax and began swinging it until he lost his balance. Old Tom then grabbed the ax and split the man's head open. Other hobos tried to stop the flow of blood by dumping a sack of flour on his head. The question in court was what actually caused the man's death. Was it the ax wound, or was it by accidentally suffocating the victim with flour? The court decided in favor of accidental death by suffocation. The Morrisey gang buried another victim of slave labor.

The average number of tramps, hobos, or bums, as the

public called them, who were held here in forced labor was about twenty at any one time. The foremen or guards usually numbered around six tough strong-looking men.

I was always afraid of the head guard by the name of Walter Quandt, a big man with heavy black hair and fierce black eyes to match, who never smiled. In one of the fracases in this den of iniquity, Quandt got shot through his neck when a prisoner wrenched his pistol away from him. A neck muscle was shot away, which caused his head to be pulled down on one side almost touching his shoulder. A face muscle was also stretched which gave him an uglier look. The rumor around at that time was that the assailant was overpowered and led away to a spot, which had been dug to bury a dead cow. A shot was heard and nothing more was ever heard about that wandering hobo. Everybody then got drunk on hard cider from the kitchen pump.

Quandt had a brother-in-law by the name of Whitbeck who was also involved at Poverty Huddle. Usually by late March money got scarce before spring planting and before the sale of horses, which were in demand for the plowing season. Whitbeck went from house to house in Fishers and bought up all the scrap lead pipe. The Morrisey farm workshop was converted for casting lead dollars and fifty cent pieces. Since the bare lead dulled rapidly upon exposure to the air, the coins were dumped into a tub of silver lacquer. My mother got one of the dollars for land rental. A dollar bought a great deal in those days, and I was sent to Jones' store for groceries. In making payment I tossed the dollar on the counter and it didn't ring. George Jones studied it carefully and declared it a counterfeit. The next thing that we heard was that Whitbeck had been arrested at his home on West Main Street in Victor and served a prison term for counterfeiting. I still have the fake dollar.

One day Old Tom drove over to the village of Rush with his enforcers and entered the local saloon. He yelled out, "I've come to rush the town and put some life into it," and with a sweep of his arm cleared the bar of all of the customers and their drinks. The reputation of the Morrisey gang was well known, and so free drinks were put up as the customers cleared out. The fire bell began to ring and men assembled. A hose was dragged through the back door and water was turned upon the unwelcome guests, who ran out the front door. There were enough men to drive them out of town.

One of the last prison breaks was made possible by some of the prisoners burning the barn to create confusion so they could escape. Later that day my brothers and sisters and I saw a man crawling down the road towards us. When we went to find out what was wrong, he said that Old Tom had broken his leg with a neck yoke, a gadget used to hitch horses to a wagon. It had taken him about five hours since the escape as he hid and later crawled the mile towards Fishers to get help.

About 1928 when Old Tom was dying in a Rochester hospital, the nurses complained that he was not housebroken. His brother, Jack, died in the springtime a couple of years later of pneumonia after sleeping during the winter on a bare concrete floor, most of the time in a drunken stupor.

The tales about the Morriseys seem endless, and many are lost because of the passing generations no longer around to relate those bizarre events which entertained me at an early age. Jack's house across the road was a part of the prison camp and has been sold and remodeled to look respectable. The main house was reduced in size and rented to a number of different families for several years. Those tenants told of hearing the echoes of tortured men around the place. The children complained of seeing strange ugly faces staring at them out of the walls. Such conditions and the superabundance of lice, bedbugs, and other vermin kept the house from steady occupancy. It was a nerve-wracking experience to live in the "Morrisey Castle."

The fiefdom of the royal family of Morrisey came to an end in July, 1952, when the house was burned in a fire drill by the Mendon Fire Department. A pile of gravel on the foundations buried the memory until recently, when new houses were built on that corner. Newcomers to this now prestigious part of Main Street, Fishers, and Mile Square Road in their wildest imaginations cannot picture what the area used to look like. Only when skeletons are discovered are they likely to believe this gory story.

Eliza O'Brien, the woman who walked the
rails for years looking for her husband
who ran away with her money.

# The Ghost of Eliza O'Brien

There are many tales of railroading on the old Auburn Road of the New York Central and Hudson River Railroad, but there is one that always haunts me. That is the pathetic story of Eliza O'Brien of Canandaigua.

Back in the pre-Civil War days, Eliza lived a normal life. She was born to modest wealth, lived near the railroad and was caught up in all of its hustle and bustle. One day, while fire wood was being loaded on a diamond-stack locomotive, she met a glamorous young man by the name of O'Brien. They fell in love and were married. After a short time he vanished, along with a good share of her money.

Eliza O'Brien was no ordinary woman but was big and strong. In a great fury of anger, she set out to find the scoundrel. She traveled to many cities and towns but never found him. As the years went by, her hatred for all men became terribly intense. Some people thought that she was crazy; but others didn't think so.

She refused to ride on trains because the engineers were men, and she felt that she was at their mercy. She even refused to eat where men were cooks. The public got to know her best as the wandering woman in hoop skirts; she walked the tracks between Rochester and Syracuse in all kinds of weather. Although always looking for her husband, she would search out women's groups and girls to lecture on the "perfidiousness of men." Maggie Murphy Ransom told me that when she went to school on Wangum Road near the creek during the Civil War, Eliza O'Brien would wait by the schoolhouse until recess time. She would take Maggie and other girls aside to tell them what nasty creatures men were and that they were the source of the world's trouble.

Families along the tracks of the Auburn Road who had no men would give Eliza a night's lodging and food. Everyone around Fishers had a great deal of sympathy for Eliza, and she claimed that this community was her second home.

The railroaders were afraid of her because of her violent temper towards men. When something went wrong or there was a train wreck, suspicion always fell upon Eliza O'Brien. There never was any real proof. No one ever dared question her. Her name became synonymous with bad luck and trouble; at those times she always seemed to be in the vicinity.

Mrs. Ransom told me about the worst train wreck she could recall. It happened on the Fishers curve just east of the station. Someone had opened a main switch, causing a head-on collision. Eliza was seen running along the tracks, before it happened, but no person could offer proof enough to make a charge.

Mrs. Ransom told me about a section gang crew riding a handcar near Camillus. They offered Eliza a ride, and she retorted, "Go away, you nasty men, and leave a 'dacent' woman alone."

After years of track-walking looking for her husband, the infirmities of old age finally stopped her grueling walks, which had lasted for days at a time. The records show that she was laid to rest in the Canandaigua Catholic Cemetery on June 14, 1893, at the age of 95 years. The railroad men breathed a sigh of relief. Nevertheless, it was short-lived, for many of the railroaders swore that they still saw her along the tracks.

One stormy night about the turn of the century, a train

full of Irish immigrants was pounding downgrade through Fishers, going west. Much to the engineer's horror, out in view of the headlight was the shadowy figure of Eliza O'Brien in her billowy hoopskirts, bobbing ahead of the locomotive but losing ground rapidly.

Blasts on the whistle would not move her. In desperation he slammed on his brakes to avoid hitting her. He ran ahead to get her off the tracks, but she was not there. Instead, he saw that the locomotive was at the brink of a huge washout at the first culvert on the Irondequoit Creek. Eliza O'Brien had saved her countrymen, regardless of the men, from a terrible wreck.

My father's brother, Henry S. Fisher, made a pencil drawing of the locomotive #701 perched on the high embankment at the end of the broken track. Everyone who saw the situation was deeply moved and puzzled.

Drawing by Henry Smith Fisher of Locomotive #701 which stopped at the edge of Culvert #1 on Irondequoit Creek adjacent to the Fisher homestead.

Numerous sightings of Eliza were reported through the years. During the summer of 1918, an engine crew left its single locomotive on the main track near the station and went into the Fishers Hotel to eat dinner. The locomotive took off by itself and nearly reached Pittsford, where it ran out of steam by the canal. Crew members were shocked not to find their locomotive when they came out. Being noon, no one was around except one person who said that an old woman was seen near the engine.

Military guards were on duty for 24 hours a day east of the station at the bridge where the Lehigh Valley Railroad goes over the Auburn tracks. No person was allowed under the bridge at night. The guards were jumpy because on certain nights they thought that they saw an old woman under the bridge who wouldn't respond when challenged. They fired warning shots, but it made no difference, for she still came back. No one told them about Eliza O'Brien.

About 1960, Elmer Sharp, who lived near the second culvert on Fisher Road, heard a crash and thought he saw an old woman near the culvert. Going over, he found that the arch of the culvert had caved in, and he went to Fowler's store to report it. The railroad, instead of making the repair, went to the New York State Public Service Commission and had the branchline, from Rochester to Canandaigua, closed permanently. Now the trackbed is used only by hikers, one of whom may still be Eliza O'Brien.

*  *  *

The first train ran on September 10, 1840 and my great-grandfather rode that train to Canandaigua. The last passenger train went through Fishers on May 18, 1959 and I took my family on that train trip.

The Railway Historical Society, on a stop at Fishers, takes the last excursion train on the Auburn Road, 1949. Note the piles of steel reinforcing mesh for the building of the New York Thruway. The Fishers Youth Band entertained.

FISHERS

# The Sign That Became a Beacon

In 1927, the flight of Charles Augustus Lindbergh across the Atlantic Ocean stimulated interest in travel by air. I saw him fly the *Spirit of Saint Louis* into the Rochester Airport after his return from Paris.

I talked to a number of pilots and found that it was not always easy for strange flyers to know what town they were flying over. That year I decided to do my part and set out to build the largest directional sign in western New York. On the broadside of our family hill I carved the sod away to letter the word "Fishers," 110 feet long and 20 feet high. I hauled up twenty loads of stone to form the letters with my one-horse wagon, and I painted these stones white.

The sign was used immediately as a part of the flight pattern to the Rochester Airport for planes arriving from Washington, Baltimore, Philadelphia and New York. Because many planes at that time did not have radio communication they relied upon landmarks. Soon an electric beam northeast-southwest, crossed the Fishers sign, and planes with radio could give their location night and day at the sign. For over fifty years the term "Holding Over Fishers" was used by the pilots calling the Rochester control tower for landing instructions. This familiar call has been replaced by a computer system. So whatever a person does, do it well, for who knows what may come of it.

# *Happy Makers*

It is very common for a person who does not understand something to dismiss it as being irrevelant. I have done this many times myself during my lifetime. However, I have also kept track of many of the things of which I have been suspicious during the years. At this point in life I find that science has explained much and that I can now accept them.

Some of these seemingly mysterious situations are the so-called energy centers found in the ground in various places. Some say that they occur in a grid pattern and can be picked up where lines from one to the other cross. In England and Europe they are called "Ley Lines." Thousands of these centers have been found in England, and in ancient times they were marked by mounds and stones, such as at Stonehenge. Some centers were used to induce fertility and healing.

It is said that anybody can locate these centers by using wires or twigs bent at right angles, walking over the ground holding them level and parallel. When an energy center is reached, they say, the wires will fly apart and that center should be approached from several directions for verification.

Of the several of which I have found and to some extent explored, two are Indian sites. Some archeologists are slow in agreeing that the Indians used these centers for therapeutic values, as was done in Europe. In every sense of the word they are "Happy Makers." One, a 1750 Seneca Indian site, which was unknowingly destroyed by the building of a dwelling at 386 Log Cabin Road was studied. It was once surrounded by a virgin forest of white pine trees—some of which are still standing—the sacred tree of the Iroquois. Excavations indicated that it was a healing center, with the fire-cracked stone from a sweat lodge and quartz crystals for healing. Indian medicine men today will tell you that hugging a white pine tree will eliminate depression and make you happy. Modern photographers have caught a flash of light at the moment a tree is hugged. A custom here has been to use a white pine tree as a radio antenna by connecting a wire to a copper nail tapped into the pine's sap line.

The second site is nearby, over the hill from 386 Log Cabin Road, is Crater Lake, a glacial kettle hole, which is believed to have had quite an effect upon the community. It was found, that when someone didn't feel good, they could hike over and spend some time by the little lake and then would come back refreshed, feeling full of good will and happiness. An energy center at this pond, it is claimed, would make a child's fine hair stand up on a clear dry day. This spot is one of the real "Happy Makers." Some say the cause of this condition is "negative ions" being emitted from the center. This condition is being duplicated by instruments now for sale. For several years negative ions have been used for healing broken bones and speeding healing after surgery. Believers say the lake center should be avoided at the beginning and during an electrical storm.

Just above Crater Lake near the boulders on the northeast side is a bowl-shaped depression. Before the undergrowth, it produced Indian artifacts, including a carved antler female figurine. Among the Iroquois these were traditionally carried by a nude female over the newly planted maize or corn fields to give them fertility. Archeologists call these little statues "September Morn" after a painting by that name. I call them "Maizees" because of their relationship with maize.

37

This is the little gray cottage on Valentown Road near Fishers, which waited forty years for Elijah and Ruby Shiling to come back. They died without returning.

# *The Mystery Cottage*

For forty years a gray cottage on Valentown Road was boarded up. My mother knew the family and their sad story. Over the years, all sorts of rumors and speculation added more mystery to the place. While some said that the owner was an eccentric, others said that a tragedy had taken place in the house and that was why no person ever tried to rent it.

In 1892 a young man by the name of Elijah G. Shilling bought a 100–acre farm on this road. By his own hands he slowly built a story and a half cottage, just right for a couple. In 1898 Elijah was ready to get married and he took for his bride Ruby Foley, daughter of Mr. and Mrs. Thomas Foley whose attractive home and enormous barn are still landmarks on their old 200–acre potato farm on Turk Hill Road.

The couple was very happy in their new home and entered into the social life of the Fishers community. "Lije," as he was affectionately called, started a seed potato and farm supply dealership near the Fishers Station. Through hard work his business prospered.

In 1906 they had a baby, who lived for only a short time. This saddened them very much. Soon after they adopted a baby girl who only lived about two years. The Shillings were devastated and they abandoned the house, leaving the dinner table set and everything else in its proper place, never again to go back into the house. They moved in with Ruby's parents on Turk Hill. Thomas Foley had a stroke and his wife became very ill; Ruby was kept quite busy.

Lije immersed himself in hard work with his farmhands on both farms. He got out of the seed potato business and became the chief supplier of potatoes for the Campbell Soup Company.

As he drove his team of horses by my house each day, he often would stop for a few moments and visit. I asked if he had any plans to sell the contents of his cottage and he said that he would sell everything to me. He had me go up to the Turk Hill house where he sold me some fine antique pieces. It was always "tomorrow" when he was going to sell me the contents of his cottage.

Elijah G. Shilling died August 7, 1947, at the age of 82, almost ten years to the day after the death of Ruby Foley Shilling. An auction to sell off the farm tools, at the Valentown Road farm, was advertised in May, 1948. I attended hoping the house would be opened.

When at the last moment the cottage door was jimmied open, everyone stood in hushed silence. No one could seem to make a bid when the chairs were first held up by the auctioneer.

I went into the cottage and saw that the table was still set, just as my mother had told me. I lifted up a plate from the dinner table. The cloth underneath was white, but everything else was black with forty years of dust. The old telephone was still on the wall with the 1908 directory, which I bought along with a few other items and the dinner set. The toys, children's furniture and personal items were taken out back and burned by the heirs.

The cottage was sold and remodeled. No longer does the lonely cottage arouse the sympathy of the passerby. The sad story has been forgotten.

# *Privy Art*

Brigham Young started it all when he wrote his name on the plaster wall of a house which he built in 1829. Today the residence is known as the Woolston-Fearnside House at 7864 Main Street, Fishers. Three years later Young quit house building and furniture making, joined the Mormons and moved west. For many years the house was used as a community hall. Traveling shows, evangelists and lecturers all left their names on the walls. During the Civil War battle pictures from magazines papered the walls.

Before Brigham Young left he was hired to build a glorified outhouse or privy in the Greek Revival architectural style. It was a miniature Parthenon with the columns supporting the entablature. Inside it could seat three adults and one child. The door was of Christian cross design. The plaster walls were stenciled with red roses; in each corner were vases to hold fresh roses when guests were visiting in order to freshen the air.

One pioneer privy was built like a small log cabin with a brick fireplace on one end in order to make it comfortable for morning and bedtime use. Some buildings were smothered over with wisteria, clemantis and honeysuckle. Interesting paths leading from the back door of the house were lined with all kinds of flowers and foxglove and tall hollyhocks surrounded a number of buildings.

A man by the name of Eberhard Potts moved to town about 1860 and entered the privy competition. His structure was designed like a turreted castle with a moat around it for convenience in cleaning in the spring. Being a man with a hip ailment, he was always seen carrying a pillow wherever he went. Therefore, it was not surprising that he built the most comfortable "one holer" in town. It was built after the style of the British throne, with a reading stand at one end. Candle sconces were mounted on the wall on both sides of the throne. When his family wanted him for some job and couldn't find him, they knew he was sitting on the throne; hence the term has passed down to this day.

The thirty-year period following the 1880s was when beautiful lithographed advertising cards were in vogue, and they provided just what was needed in covering the privy walls with a collage of brilliant pictures. Colored post cards, valentines, and holiday cards were put to good use.

In many homes it became a fad to have a room decorated with names, pictures and colorful advertising cards. All of the houses on one street were thus decorated. However, it was the privy which received the most special attention until it became a status symbol to have the most outstanding privy in town.

The hotel did not go in for artistic improvements, but the Haileys, Fowlers, Van Voorhis, O'Briens, Fords, Sullivans and many others, who are forgotten, did. It was Clara Fisher who usually rated the best. William and Addie Fisher had their Greek Revival outhouse papered with classic French wallpaper.

When Valentown Hall was opened by Levi Valentine in 1879 as a shopping plaza and comunity center, the stairways and top floor ballroom walls were where you registered your name. The Valentown privys for both men and women had brilliant colored cloth pasted to the walls. Levi had the privy interior—of his other grocery store at the corner of Fowler and Railroad Streets—all stenciled with valentine hearts.

This fad of registering and decorating passed away as the family guest book came into vogue. One family kept for years a special tablecloth for dinner guests to sign. It was great for stimulating table conversation about people who had dined there before.

Once a week, Cynthia Durham carried the mail from the central
Post Office in Canandaigua to the new Rochester Post Office
(1812–1815).

# Bears, Wolves and the U.S. Mail

The lifeline of Central and Western New York was the Great Genesee Highway, built in 1794 across the state as a military highway to Avon. This is now known as Route 5. It penetrated a wilderness with many dangers, including wolves, bears, mountain lions and rattlesnakes. Nevertheless, civilization with all of its benefits moved in to tame the frontier.

Canandaigua and Geneva were the important outposts. From here mail was distributed to a wide area. When Colonel Nathaniel Rochester was establishing his village at the Falls of the Genesee, he needed mail service. On November 19, 1812, through the kindness of his intimate friend, Henry Clay, Colonel Rochester got a commission of appointment for Abelard Reynolds as Postmaster for Rochester. The office was at his home on the enclosed front porch. It is now the site of Reynold's Arcade. At the same time a contract was made with Gershom Dunham of Penfield to carry the mail on horseback between Rochester and Canandaigua once a week, a distance of more than 30 miles.

A sudden sickness prevented Gershom from carrying out his part of the contract, and so his wife, Cynthia, rode the mail route for several years. Her stops are known today as Centerfield, Holcomb, East Bloomfield, Victor, Fishers, and Pittsford. When she arrived at some stops, men would announced, "Here comes the *fe-mail!*"

Cynthia was my second great-grandmother and many stories have been passed down, along with her saddlebag and personal letters. They tell of how she was given up for lost during the severe winter of 1813–14, but survived because of the warmth of her horse's body. During another storm, when food was scarce in the wilds, a wolf pack chased Cynthia for miles in an attempt to kill her horse. By the use of a long birch rod, she was able to lash the wolves when they got too close and tried to tear the leg tendons of the horse.

Once, on what is now Fisher Road, her trotting horse made a sudden lunge forward in time to escape the pounce of a mountain lion waiting on an overhanging tree limb. Another time, when the weather was bad, she stayed overnight in a deserted cabin. Another night she spent with a family whose bed was infested with bedbugs and on a wilderness trail a mother bear with a cub attacked her.

After his health improved, Gershom had many similar experiences when he carried the mail. He provided messenger service and did small shopping errands for the forest families along the way. Gershom held many town offices in Penfield and later in Fairport when he moved there. As a deacon in the Congregational Church, he was empowered to do marriage ceremonies on his mail route. He gained fame as "the marrying mailman." He drew up legal papers and lent money. His name appears on many area deeds as a witness.

Gershom was thrown from his horse when charged by a bear at the Fisher homestead, but escaped by climbing a tree about 100 feet east of the house. I heard this event talked about in my youth. The same situation again overtook him opposite the Or-ring Stone Tavern, now the Stone-Tolan House, on East Avenue in Brighton. There he was able to climb upon the historic Indian Council Rock. This family story was verified by the late A. Emerson

Babcock, the Brighton Town Historian and Town Supervisor.

As late as 1845, when the Auburn & Rochester Railroad made possible daily mail delivery, mail was taken from the Fishers office on horseback to Mendon, Mendon Center, Honeoye Falls and North Bloomfield. Tyler Squires, who lived near the station, had the mail contract. Twice a bear forced the horse and rider over the cliff into Irondequoit Creek on West Main Street, Fishers.

Helen Jane Pardee Fisher had bear trouble after she came as a bride in 1850 to live at the Fisher homestead. She was noted for her pies and cookies. The pies, with their delightful aroma, were normally placed in the open pantry window to cool. When she began missing pies, she put the blame on the neighborhood boys, who stoutly denied the charge. Thus one day after baking a number of pies, she again placed them in the window and laid in wait. She heard a clawing sound and discovered bear's paws reaching in for the pies. She slammed the window down on the hungry bear's paws, and since then no bear has ever come back to the Fisher homestead. This window is still an interesting curiosity to the many youthful Fisher descendants.

# The Strange Experience
# of Bertha Connelly

Fred Connelly and his beautiful wife, Bertha Carpenter, lived with their daughter, Thelma, in a very attractive house next to the Fishers Post Office. Behind the house and Post Office stood their seed potato warehouse, a coal chute, and farm supply buildings. Fred managed these businesses for his widowed mother, Sarah Murphy Connelly, who was also the Postmaster in Fishers.

Bertha Connelly was a very charming and outgoing person and a leader in the social life of the community. In 1916 Fred died suddenly. My father, with his elegant surrey-with-the-fringe-on-top, carried the pall bearers in the procession to the Mendon Cemetery. I watched the funeral cortege with its horse-drawn black hearse.

Bertha then took a bookkeeping job with the old Locke Insulator Company in Victor. She commuted for a time by train before moving in with her father, Frank Carpenter, to East Main Street, Victor.

On Christmas Day, 1917, all of the family relatives gathered in the Fishers home of Sarah Connelly. Bertha was entertaining at the piano and then suddenly played and sang in a sobbing manner the song "Memories." This emotionally broke up the family gathering.

On January 3, 1918, nine days later, she went out of the Insulator office at quitting time as usual with the girls. There stood Fred Connelly, who had been dead for two years. Bertha was quite stunned, and the others heard her say, "Why, Fred, what are you doing here?" "I have come to get you," he replied, and then disappeared. The news of this spread rapidly all over Victor and Fishers.

The next morning, January 4th, she was sick and called Dr. Alfred Mead. The day after she died of what was listed on her death certificate as pneumonia. The day Bertha was dying, her father, Frank Carpenter, pleaded with her to hang on and live for the sake of her daughter, Thelma. She said that she couldn't because Fred was coming for her. Her father died in the morning, and Bertha died in the afternoon. A double funeral was held.

Later that year the killer disease, called Spanish Influenza, killed thirteen people in Fishers including the Postmaster, Sarah Connelly, and Fred Connelly's brother-in-law, George P. Fowler, the storekeeper.

# Short Circuit That Started a Multi-Million Dollar Industry

"Would you please send someone over to the station and wake up that lazy Fred Locke? He has not reported the last two passenger trains."

This was the message sent in 1896 by the Rochester train dispatcher to the Fishers telephone operator, Lillian Wiley, later Mrs. Lillian Leahy. A messenger was paid the usual ten cents a trip to bring Fred Locke to the phone at the operator's office on Fowler Street. He vowed to the train dispatcher that he was awake and that he had reported the trains properly, as told to me by Mrs. Leahy.

This same situation was happening to other telegraph operators along the Auburn Road of the New York Central Railroad. Fred Locke investigated to see what the problem was and found that when it rained or during an ice storm, the electric wires shorted out at the poles. He found a type of glass insulator, which would prevent low voltage wires from shorting in a rain storm. He then became an agent for that company and so solved the telegraph problem, but not the transmission of high voltage electric power.

Mrs. Leahy remembered how Charles Webster, a talented mechanic, was approached to solve the power line problem. He was the son-in-law of Kingsley Brownell, the owner and operator of the old Fisher mill near the station. A deal was made and sealed with a handshake that Webster would turn out on a lathe patterns for a number of prototype porcelain insulators. The first lot of insulators was made in King Brownell's mill, using clay from a nearby hill to make the brown glaze. When they were thoroughly dried, Fred took them to his home on Dryer Road near the Victor railroad station and baked them in his wife's kitchen oven.

There was so much interest in the new insulator that a place was needed to do the manufacturing. The ideal place at the time was the Brownell mill. Old King was furious with his tinkering son-in-law and ordered the project out and refused to sell his property.

In 1897 a group financed Fred Locke by buying the Wilbur Coal & Lumber Company next to the Victor railroad station (where insulators are still being manufactured today). I have the papers that were drawn up for Brownell to sell water power to the Locke Insulator Plant four miles away in Victor. Even though a generator was made to order, old King refused to let it be used at his mill.

Brownell's Mill, circa 1912, built in 1890,
was built on land purchased from Charles Fisher in 1869.

When the Victor plant was established, Charles Webster was forgotten as a partner. He then went into another business buying the first used cars and reconditioning them for sale. I loved to watch those cars being tried out on the hill in front of our house, especially those with a single cylinder, which were called "one-lungers" because of the sound when the motor was running.

I used to visit with old King Brownell who knew about the local history. I asked him why he objected so to the insulator project. He said he told Locke that his insulators could never make as much money as his mill was making and that he would never even consider being a partner with his son-in-law. Even though he was proven wrong, old King would never admit it. Before he died on June 19, 1924, old King gave me the wood lathe used by Louis P. Locke and also some of the wooden patterns for those first insulators. Both the mill and the lathe had belonged to my great-grandfather, Charles Fisher, before he sold them to King Brownell. Louis P. Locke, who married my cousin, gave me his father's famous telegraph key for my collection. Along with my Locke items are some of his first insulators, so marked and baked under the glaze. Some of this type were among the first used by the Rochester and Eastern Rapid Railway, a trolley line running between Rochester and Geneva in 1903. Later the development of the Niagara River Power Project required Locke Insulators.

James L. Locke, Fred's youngest son, wrote me a letter in 1962 to put with my files about his father.

> My father came to Victor in 1888 as agent for the Auburn Road (NYC)—there were 14 passenger trains each day in addition to freight. Mother, Mercie Peer Locke, learned the Morse Code and helped father to "OS" trains (this is, report arrival and departure) so he could get in a few extra

hours on his new invention. Father, admired the inventors Field, Bell, and Edison, and in 1890 made Victor's first electric lamp. He made a small generator and attached it to the steam engine at Eugene Barry's flour mill and lighted the room (now The Whistlestop Restaurant). Father purchased the first telephones in Victor in 1903 and connected his home to the factory."

Although the Locke Insulator Company was doing a booming business, Fred lost control in 1909 to Rochester bankers. He then built a new company in Lima, now the Pinco Insulator plant. He was also involved with the Lapp Insulator Company in LeRoy.

In 1970 Brent Mills, the retired president of that company and author of a history of insulators, wrote me the following:

'Fred Locke was, indeed, the telegraph operator at Fishers. I must have heard John Lapp tell the story twenty times, that Fred Locke was the operator at Fishers Corners, described as a small town just outside of Victor. So, you see, the only thing that I have to go on is John Lapp's words, though I am certain I am not mistaken about them. Regarding the message that did not come through, I don't believe this was any specific signal, but rather a characteristic situation that developed every time it rained.

Mr. Mills had a museum collection for the Lapp Company of early insulators but did not have any of those first made by Locke. I gave him several.

Since so much misinformation has been published about the first making of the porcelain insulators, I felt interviewing those who were involved would make the best record. Mrs. Lillian Leahy was my best informant on the Locke story, for she lived close to all of the events. In her later life she worked as an expert in the ceramic laboratory of the then Victor Insulators, Inc. She told me that Fred Locke himself personally hauled wagon loads of red clay from our Fisher farm hill to make the brown insulator glaze.

Mr. Locke, with his helper Louis A. Crowley, in 1907 accidently uncovered the grave of Pabos, a previously unknown early American explorer, which had in it a stone marker dated June 10, 1618. In commemoration, I built nearby the nine-foot high stone pyramid to Pabos.

"General" Ulysses Grant Hunt of Fishers, New York.

# The Man With the
# Healing Touch

"General" Ulysses Grant Hunt was more than a farmer. He was an outdoors man who loved to hunt, fish and study nature. He was also respectfully known as "the man with the healing touch."

When Ulysses Hunt was born on November 29, 1854, in Fishers, boys from Fishers were sending letters back from Forts Henry and Donelson, Shiloh, Vicksburg and Chattanooga, and were praising the victorious General Ulysses Simpson Grant. So it is not surprising that Charles Wesley Hunt and his wife, Martha Baldwin, named the ninth of their sixteen children after this man. Although nicknamed "General," he never served in any military capacity. General Hunt always had a kind expression with a bronzed healthy tinge to his skin, which was accentuated by exposure to the weather. Expert hunters and fishermen sought his company and took him on hunting trips to other states. Very few men could outshoot him.

One of General Hunt's attributes was cooking, for which he was equally famous. When the Fishers firemen put on a dinner, it was General who did the cooking. Once a year General Hunt and George Proseus would gather up the local boys for a week's trip to Honeoye Lake. In the autumn all boys were notified that if they would stay out of his melon patch, he would put on a harvest feast for them. This became a great event and was held for a number of years. After the General stopped farming, the tradition was continued by Roy Battams, who owned the farm adjoining on the hill above.

The General was guide and host to many nature lovers. While he was active, the nationally-famous naturalist and author John Burroughs would pay a visit to General Hunt for botanizing in the woods and swamps around Fishers. Shelley Crumb of Pittsford would always be a member of the party, along with his neighbor and relative, Frederick Boughton, who was an expert on mushrooms. General would show that group where the rare orchids grew, but he would not show me. He was afraid that they would be dug up and lost, as they eventually were. Each spring General would share the beauty of the georgeous pink orchid by cutting only one slip for display in Fowler's store.

When General Hunt's father died in 1898 at age 78, it fell to General to nurse his ailing mother for the seven more years she lived. It was at this time that he discovered his unusual gift of a healing touch, which made him in demand as a private nurse. His healing was in no way connected with faith healing, for he never was involved with religion. He communed with God in nature.

When any family was in trouble, he always made himself available. The General would move his hands over the ailing parts of the human body, sometimes touching, and other times where the condition was bad, he left both palms down on the spot. He claimed that he was passing along electrical healing charges to the patient.

One of his most talked about successes was when his nephew, Walter Smith, was taken to the hospital in Canandaigua with a ruptured appendix in the days before the wonder drugs. The doctors said that there was no hope for him. General Hunt went to his bed and stayed all night. Dr. Alfred Armstrong came

James O'Rourke (alias Jim Riley) standing by his well-used old kitchen stove in his log cabin at Fishers.

in the next morning expecting to find him dead, but declared Walter past the crisis. He told General that what he did for the patient was more than the medical profession could do.

One winter before World War I, James O'Rourke, better known as Jim Riley, who lived in the 1790 log cabin at the end of Log Cabin Road, became very sick, as did several gypsies living there. General Hunt was called over next door to nurse the sick.

In a reasonable length of time they were all well again.

Jim's father had been a blacksmith in New York City and had shod the horses owned by the gypsies. When the blacksmith died, the gypsies brought up his son, Jim. He traveled with them all over the country. When the gypsy king died, Jim married the very attractive queen. After she died, Jim decided to settle down in Fishers and stop roaming and he bought the old log cabin. He did not, however, sever his gypsy ties but allowed a good-sized band to spend each winter with him. I will never forget the colorful sight of the long caravan of European gypsy wagons leaving town. There were bunk wagons, loads of hay, wagons loaded with tents, wagons with cooking equipment hanging on the side, and large kettles hanging underneath. Horses were ridden and extra horses were tethered behind wagons and buggies. What helped make the parade so colorful were the brightly clothed people.

The friendly and neighborly figure of "General" Ulysses Grant Hunt has been sadly missed since he passed away on August 9, 1939.

# *The Fairy Farm*

Four acres of land all aglow and above it fireflies appearing to dance up and down was enough to shake the nerves of an Irishman coming from the "Ol Sod." This is the way it was for years at the end of Lower Fishers Road at Log Cabin Road. The spectacle attracted many people who named it the Fairy Farm.

It all started when Charles Fisher bought a farm on February 2, 1855 in lot 37 of the fourth range to connect his thousand acres of valley farms. He needed the heavy growth of virgin pine and hemlock trees to supply lumber orders for his sawmill. In clearing the land for cultivation, he exposed a good depth of rich muckland and decayed wood. During cultivation afterwards the soil gave off a phosphorescent glow in the dark.

Many Irish families were moving into the area to work on the railroad. In Ireland they had grown up in the traditional home of fairies and leprechauns in the glow of the peat bogs. Here was the same phosphorescent glow. Many of the Irish just laughed about the superstitions while others were serious.

Alexander McCrahon and his wife, Bridget, came from Ireland in the summer of 1849 and moved into the Fairy Farm house, where their youngest child, Michael, was born that same year. They lived there until after the Civil War, but there are no records about the McCrahons and the fairies.

Alexander got a job as an engineer on the railroad, however, the railroad did not hire son Edward, so he took a job selling Rochester nursery stock in Louisiana. The Confederate 7th

McCrahon House, Log Cabin Road, Fishers.

Louisiana Volunteers were recruiting Irish boys for military service and so he joined unbeknownst to his family. About the same time son Alexander joined the Union 108th regiment in Rochester.

After the war, when the brothers came home, they found that they had fought opposite each other at Antietam and at Gettysburg, where Edward was wounded, Alexander had been firing a cannon from 50 yards away on the opposite side.

Before Antietam, Edward was made Aid-de-camp to General Thomas "Stonewall" Jackson, and was among the staff on April 30, 1862 when Jackson made Lewiston his headquarters. Lewiston was the family home of Mr. and Mrs. Samuel Hance Lewis, the grandparents of this author's wife, Lillian Lewis Fisher, and she remembers the story that "Stonewall" Jackson slept in bed with his boots on and grandmother Lewis didn't like that at all. After the war Edward was always known as Stonewall McCrahon.

The Irish who worked at the mill built a covered bridge

over Irondequoit Creek to connect Lower Fishers Road across the fields to Fisher Road. A glacial boulder with a strange shape resembling a man's head was in the path of the road. Orders were to get rid of it. The Irish objected to its being moved. They didn't even want to get near it. With the stone face staring at them this was definitely the headquarters of the leprechauns. To disturb them could bring harm to the person or their families, it was believed.

As time went on quite a controversy built up about the stone obstruction. Later, a mule team finally rolled the stone out of the way. Fairies are supposed to protect their homesites—the boulder was back in its old spot the next morning. No one professed knowledge as to how it got back. It had to have been done by the fairies, they said. This movement of the boulder back and forth took place several times and then one night the boulder disappeared. It never came out whether the fairies did it or if it was done by those who wanted it removed.

I discussed the fairy situation with Jim Sullivan, and he said that he was not a superstitious man and made a joke about the fairy farm. However, in his last days when he was disposing of his property, a gypsy fortune teller came to his house and told him that he had only two years to live. A friend wanted to buy a building lot. The way Jim decided upon the price was that since the field normally produced a certain profit in one year, and since he had two years to live, double that amount and that was the price which he charged for the building lot.

After the year 1900, Homer J. Hill of the pioneer Hill family of Fishers bought the Fairy Farm. He married Frances Buckley, a neighbor girl whose parents came from Ireland. They were strong believers in fairies and leprechauns. The Buckleys had lived on the Wilkins farm, an adjoining Fisher property, where there were many fairy rings and fireflies. A fairy ring is a circle of toadstools where the leprechauns do their dances. A person should never step in the center of them, for the little people might get injured. Each year these rings get larger, expanding until something gets in their way, such as a building or a road.

Jim Sullivan was amused about how the Buckleys followed all of the rules of the homeland to co-exist with the little people. Their summers were spent indoors in the evening when the fairies were flashing their little lanterns on the lawn and in the high grass; the American fireflies upset them.

Homer Hill continued to cultivate the flatlands across the creek, as was done by previous farmers. The land still gave off a glow. It bothered Mrs. Hill, or "Frankie," as she was called. Homer refused to let his wife stop him from growing crops in the field, even if the horses did step on a few leprechauns. He compromised by keeping the cattle in the barnyard at night. Frankie's fear was that if the little people were injured, they might retaliate by causing deformed calves or even bring about a milk shortage.

Homer maintained a stable of fine race horses and he took prizes at the old Rochester Driving Park and at other famous tracks. Trouble did erupt between Frankie and Homer when he built his practice race track on part of the controversial fairy field. While the team graders were building the track, Frankie threw herself on the ground in front of the graders. The track was built, nevertheless, and used during bright daylight hours.

About the time the Hills moved to the Fairy Farm, their daughter Mae was born. As they lived in a spot surrounded by fairy habitations they had to take the utmost caution. The danger was that if fairies got into the house, they could cause considerable harm. Well, it happened one night. The doors and windows were accidently left open on a hot night. Baby Mae cried violently and Frankie was sure that the spirites had injured her. It was not long afterward that they found out that the baby was mentally retarded. Ever after no door or window was left open when the fairies were dancing. It was annoying for evening callers to be told to come in the daytime.

After Homer Hill died, Frankie and Mae continued to live in the house fenced in by their restrictive superstitions. Besides farming and horsebreaking, Homer had supplemented his income by cutting his willow trees and then sawing them into blanks to be carved into finished wooden legs for amputees. He had flooded the market with wooden legs and still had a barn full of blanks. These legs had to be stacked in a certain manner to help the wood season properly. Frankie was very upset, for she claimed that the leprechauns were restacking the wooden legs, making them unsalable.

Hungry times set in, so she began operating a distillery to sell moonshine. It was powerful stuff, for I saw many men lying along the road completely unable to walk. One day the still set the barn afire and the neighbors tried to put it out. I was not there, but it was described to me as a comical mess.

The firefighters were more concerned about saving the whiskey than the barn. Instead of a bucket brigade line from the creek to the barn, each person who was not prostrate on the ground carried pails of water where he thought it would do the most good. Several pairs of boots were in use but many persons each had only one boot on. Some of those on the roof with a boot on should have been down at the creek. Frankie was also on the roof of her house with a horsewhip, trying to drive off the firefighters because the barn fire would drive the fairies and little people into the house through the open windows. Pails of alcoholic liquid splashed onto the fire only made it burn faster.

The house was not saved by the firefighters. It was saved because the wind was blowing the embers in another direction. What disappeared were the covered bridge, the picturesque red barn, the distillery, and a heap of blank wooden legs. The Hill family is no more, but as to the fairies and leprechauns, perhaps one may still find them there.

# *Guarding Troop Trains*

When the United States entered World War I on April 6, 1917, the New York State National Guard was mustered into the Regular Army and sent to France. A statewide Home Defense Reserve was organized in order to fill the gap for any emergency. Six companies were organized for Ontario County. Fishers Company F, totaling 70 fully trained men, was organized and captained by my father, Almon Preston Fisher, and included ten underage, junior-grade members that included this writer.

For two years Fishers was like an armed camp. The weekly drills and guard duty on the railroad bridges and culverts kept us busy. Every few days troop trains were moving over the New York Central Railroad and the Lehigh Valley Railroad. These trains had to be protected, for they carried no arms.

Honeoye Falls and other area companies came here for maneuvers and parades. Several fully-equipped sham battles were held in other villages of the county, with all companies participating. Money was raised weekly by dances at Valentown Hall. Every so often a formal military ball was held, with all of the decorum and changing of the guards.

Word was received at the station when a troop train was expected through. If there was time, we walked the tracks or patrolled in both directions. It was surprising the amount of sabotaged tracks and switches we found! In order to stop this a single pilot engine went ahead, which was supposed to be the victim to be wrecked instead of the troop train. We would plant

Members of the First New York Dragoons, a re-activated Civil War Cavalry regiment from Fishers on target line.

three track torpedoes a short distance apart, used as a warning of danger. For caution only, two torpedoes would be attached to the track.

Being halfway between Rochester and Canandaigua, the sidings at Fishers had over a mile and half of tracks. This meant that east- and west-bound trains were able to pass here. We were busy with troop trains but this also gave us a chance to pass out apples and fruit to the soldiers.

One particular troop train took the siding for another train to pass. In the open vestibules between each coach were machine guns aimed at each door and a machine gun on the end coach. The train was loaded with recalcitrant draftees who didn't want to go to war. They planned to jump the train at any stop if they could. Our armed company was strung along both sides of the track when the train came to a stop. Later, I became friends with Kenneth Bradford Burns who was the engineer of that troop train. When that train reached Geneva, the men rioted inside of the coaches and tried to climb out of the windows, but a few warning shots stopped that, according to Mr. Burns.

When the armistice was signed on November 11, 1918, I gathered up the records, flag, bugle, some uniforms, and a number of guns, along with a host of memories, to be saved for the future. As of February 1987, I became the sole survivor of Company F.

Miles Cutting, early photographer, miller, Postmaster
of Railroad Mills, and shipper of flour.

# *Train Robbery Attempt*

From the Rochester Herald, Friday, October 30, 1893:
To Rob a Train
Tramps Pile Ties on Central Tracks
Charles Brazee, a One-armed Man,
Discovers Obstruction at Railroad Mills,
And with Postmaster Cutting Warns
Passenger Train.

Train #1 on Auburn Branch of the Central in Rochester at 9:25 p.m. was brought to a stop with a violent jerk a short distance west of Fishers last night. Engineer Mason H. Gibson of 35 Grand Avenue, this city, was at the levers. His attention had been attracted by the waving of a lantern just ahead on this track, and the readiness with which he responded to the danger signal threw the passengers from their seats.

Conductor James Potter of 205 Central Avenue, was in charge of the train. When it came to a stop he walked to the location and there met two men who were laboring under intense excitement and narrating to the engineer the story of an attempt to wreck the train. The men were Postmaster Miles S. Cutting of Railroad Mills and Charles Brazee, a one-armed tramp from Auburn.

Brazee, in the tourist's parlance, was 'pounding the ties' over the Auburn Road to Rochester, when about a mile west of Fishers he came upon a pile of ties built up in a pyramid form upon the tracks. A train striking it from either side would surely be derailed. Brazee, with his one arm, was powerless so far as clearing the tracks was concerned, so he ran for assistance.

The nearest house was that of Postmaster Cutting. He listened to the tramp's story, then grabbing a lighted lantern, ran down the track with Brazee, succeeded in stopping the train and doubtless saving many lives. The obstruction was placed in a ravine 25 feet deep and at one of the worst curves on the road. Notwithstanding this fact, the train was making a mile a minute and would have met with terrible destruction but for the timely warning.

About 150 people from Auburn and stations east were on the train. When they learned of their narrow escape from horrible death or injury, there was great excitement. They were all sure that the train had been held up by robbers and that they must turn over their money and valuables. While the object doubtless was to wreck and plunder the train, no bold robbers put in an appearance. They had intended to rob the dead and injured, but their plans were frustrated.

One kind faced young father, carrying an infant in arms, went to the platform of the car to learn the reason for the abrupt stop. When he heard it, his face blanched, and he ran back into the coach, handed the child over to another man and said in a husky voice, "Pard, take my baby, we are going to have a tough time getting away from here alive. We are held up by desperadoes and might as well give up our money and let them go."

Miss Rossford of Canandaigua, who is employed in an office on State Street, this city, had been spending Sunday at her house and was returning to Rochester on the train. She took off her gold watch and hid it with her purse under the seat. Nearly all the other passengers did likewise, expecting every moment the robbers would board the train.

One old man, said to be a Canandaigua farmer, opened his carpet bag, took out a roll of greenbacks, smoothed them out, and deposited them carefully between his throbbing pate and brown wig. He would have been safe in the presence of the late Jesse James. A young lady, with rare presence of mind, stowed her valuables away in her stocking.

After a delay of twenty minutes, the ties were removed from the track by the trainmen and passengers, and the train rolled on its way without incident. Brazee says that as he approached the obstruction, he heard several men hurrying away through an adjacent woods. He did not see the men. It is said that several tramps were arrested near the scene of the attempted wreck yesterday. Detectives are looking for a clue to the perpetrators of the fiendish act.

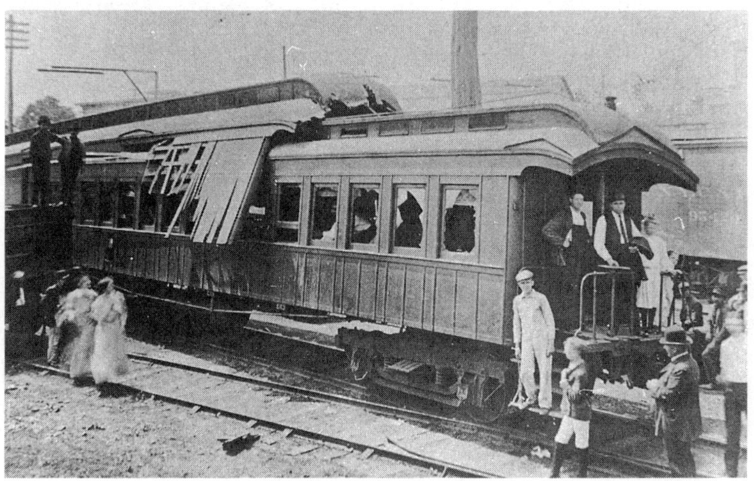

Train wreck near Railroad Mills where Miles Cutting was killed.

Mace Gibson, the man in charge of the engine, is a veteran in the employ of the Central road and has grown gray in the service. He was about the coolest man on the train last night, though in the most dangerous position. Conductor Potter said that he expected robbers would board the train, and alighted from it with the determination of fighting for his life and the lives of the passengers, one of whom was his wife. No great amount of valuables was in transportation.

* * *

Ralph B. Southgate, nephew of Miles Cutting (who was present during the train robbery), made the following comments:

The police, upon interrogating Charles Brazee more thoroughly, concluded that he was not telling the true story of the train wrecking attempt, and accused him of placing the ties on the track. He was accordingly charged with the crime, arrested, tried in court and sent to prison.

Miles Cutting was born in England, came to America, and joined his uncle, John Cutting, who operated the Wanghum Mills in Fishers and a large flour mill at Railroad Mills. The mill was burned to the ground on July 14, 1883. It was replaced by a small grist mill, now unused, which is still standing on the site of the larger mill.

Mr. Cutting died in June, 1907, the victim by a quirk of fate of a train accident near the site of the attempted wreck of 1893. It was also on the almost identical site where Cutting's wife was killed and he was badly injured in a wreck about 20 years before. On the night on which he was killed, Cutting was homeward bound from Rochester when his train collided head-on with a freight train on the single track line between Cartersville on the Erie Canal and Railroad Mills.

# *An Unexpected Scoop*

Oldtime transportation used to be "dangerous to your health." The strap iron rails spiked to wooden supports came loose and shot up through the passenger coaches, sometimes impaling a passenger to the ceiling. There were train wrecks galore. Passenger trains were even stuck in snowbanks for days. So a train ride was often the epitome of adventure. Such events were not recorded in ballads immortalizing the tales of area railroading as was done about the nearby Erie Canal.

One area event back in January, 1885, however, captured the national fancy. No one before had ever seen a locomotive riding *pickaback* on top of another. This happened not far from here on the Batavia and Canandaigua Railroad, known jokingly as the "Peanut Branch" of the New York Central and Hudson River Railroad.

During that January a very heavy snowstorm blanketed the whole region. Engineer Walling convinced the train dispatcher at Canandaigua that his high-wheel-drive Engine #295 could easily get through the snowdrifts to make the fifty miles to Batavia, therefore, train #61 with about a half load of passengers bravely left at 6:10 p.m. on schedule. At Wheeler's station by Mud Creek traveling was getting tough. At Holcomb several passengers were discharged, and the agent questioned the continuation of the trip. Near Ionia the train got hopelessly buried in a snowdraft. Since the train was overdue at West Bloomfield, the Ionia agent telegraphed for help from both Canandaigua and Batavia. It was a desperate situation with no possibility for an extra snowplow,

This photograph appeared in the December 26, 1936
edition of the *Rochester Times-Union*.

because several trains were snowbound between Fishers and Pittsford on the Auburn Road and on the Main Line near Palmyra.

The next day, while the blizzard was still raging, a plow became available at Batavia. In the meantime, the overnight passengers had found shelter at nearby farms. Conductor Michael McIntyre was placed in charge of two locomotives to push the snowplow to the rescue. McIntyre drove head engine #213, and Engineer George Acker, Sr., operated booster engine #470.

With those high-speed drive wheels in action, no drift was considered an obstacle. LeRoy, Caledonia and Honeoye Falls were passed with ease, but still no snowbound train. Then someplace between West Bloomfield and Ionia during the blinding storm was heard a deafening crash and the sound of grinding steel. When the weather cleared, it was found that the westbound passenger high-wheel-drive engine #295 had been scooped up and had landed on top of the booster second engine #470. The snowplow had not only cleared away the drift and scooped up the passenger engine, but also had pushed the baggage-mail car and two passenger coaches off the single track railroad. No record can be found listing injuries.

In the process of cleaning up the mess, it was found best to tow the doubledecker locomotive to the Batavia railroad yard where mechanical means could be used to separate the two locomotives. Everything was fine until they came to a low overhead bridge at Batavia. The conglomeration had to be towed to a sand pit to await spring when the ground was not frozen. Teams of horses pulled scoops of sand and buried the bottom engine #470 until the top engine #295 was on ground level. It was then easily removed with teams of horses and mules.

Photographer P. B. Housekneiht of 106 Main Street in Batavia did a flourishing business selling photographs of the accident in all of the towns along the line. Within the past decade the Erie Railroad published this picture, saying this accident happened on their railroad.

# A Baby Betrothal

One hundred years ago extra land simply was not available locally. Potato growers were at the threshold of fifty years of a very prosperous business. No extra land could be purchased.

Two of the largest landholders figured that they had the sure-fire answer to the problem of land shortage. Although it would not be of immediate help, it would be ideal for their next generation, who certainly would have the same problem. The scheme was to join their adjacent farms by marriage, but this was not going to be possible until some children were born.

Peter Simmons Bonesteele had a son, P. Frank Bonesteele, born July 2, 1872. Peter had over 200 acres of rich potato lands and had tried to buy more without success.

E. Reece Reed married Charlotte Parks on January 24, 1871, and became the man in charge of the Parks Place with 200 acres of land between Main Street, Fishers, and the boundary of the Bonesteele farm. They had a daughter, Irma, born April 28, 1881. About 400 acres of the Parks land had already been given to heirs; the chances of getting any of it back were hopeless.

Reece Reed and Peter Bonesteele made a serious agreement and sealed it with a handshake to have Irma and Frank marry after college. If the same deal could be carried out for the following generations with other adjacent landowners, of course assisted by birth control to limit the children to one, a monopoly of land and wealth could be built up under the Bonesteele name.

The baronial mansion was already built and was, and is,

perhaps the finest house in the town. Peter's father, Philip P. Bonesteele, had it built during the years 1832 to 1835. William Ayling was the mason who built it of cobblestones, and the lumber was sawed in Charles Fisher's mill. Social events were held in the second floor ballroom on the north wing. Peter's dream of a landed estate would have been very unusual if everything went as planned.

However, on August 17, 1881, Peter Bonesteele died just four months after Irma Reed was born. Did death break the contract? No! Frank's mother, Octavious Morgan Bonesteele, kept the agreement in force.

In 1894 Frank was sent to the Massachusetts Institute of Technology to study architecure. In his third year, a crop failure at home prevented him from finishing college. He took a job with a firm of architects in Boston. Frank met a very talented instructor in the field of physics and astronomy at the Cambridge School for Girls, a Boston preparatory school for college. Her name was Sarah Abigail Hall and she was of Pilgrim ancestry. Frank upset his mother and the Reed family by announcing his marriage to Sarah on September 4, 1898, thus breaking the betrothal agreement of the parents.

Eleven years later Irma Reed married an ingenious inventor by the name of Louis P. Locke. He was the son of Fred M. Locke, the inventor of the porcelain insulator, which made possible the high tension transmission lines for electric power. Neither Irma Locke nor Sarah Bonesteele had children.

Frank and Sarah went on their wedding trip to Iowa, where they inspected land owned by his parents before returning to supervise the operation of the Bonesteele farm. It was a sharp change of life for Sarah to live in this quiet rural community. In

Boston she had been associated with such people as Alexander Graham Bell, Mark Twain and a host of prominent educators. Just the year before her marriage she had the unusual experience of teaching physics and astronomy to Helen Keller, who was blind and speechless.

The new Mrs. Bonesteele discontinued the select social parties and balls of Peter Bonesteele's day; she brought a new brand of culture to the community. National figures were house guests, and they were introduced to the Fishers community. Jessie Bonesteele/Bonstell, the world-famous actress and the head of her own acting company, was a cousin. Jessie was graduated from the nearby Valentown School of Acting in 1883. Sarah opened her home for meetings on scientific subjects and she herself lectured in the open on astronomy. Out of the attic came the weaving looms and the tools of pioneer crafts which she taught. She gained considerable fame as a weaver and collector of early American coverlets.

Frank Bonesteele died June 6, 1919, and his mother, Mrs. Peter Bonesteele, died December 6, 1927. Sarah sold the farm in 1946 when old age crept upon her and moved to Chicago to take care of her brother. She died there August 22, 1947, thus ending an interesting chapter of local history. A new chapter was started with the building and opening in October, 1971, of the gigantic Eastview Mall in Bonesteele's potato field opposite their mansion. The house is now being used as the Cobblestone Art Center—Sarah Hall Bonesteele's theme is being carried on.

# The Phantom Train

The passenger trains on the Lehigh Valley Railroad are no more, but there is still one that the train dispatcher never knew about. Locally, it is called the "Ghost Train." Originally, it was a crack passenger train, the Lehigh Limited, listed as train #6 out of Buffalo.

On the night of September 11, 1905, two young men in a horse and carriage were killed at the Wangum Road crossing in Fishers. They were Augustus H. Frank, age 26, and John Flynn, age 22. A party was in progress at a home south of Fishers, but these two boys decided to come home early. Ernest Barry was supposed to have ridden with them, but he had a premonition that he should not, and so he lived to raise a family.

It was a semi-foggy night when the train roared over the crossing, smashing the buggy, and killing the horse and riders. Fog often hangs in layers over the tracks westward of the crossing, especially around nine o'clock when the accident happened. Through the years many people have parked their cars at the Wangum Road crossing to watch for this strange phenomena to reoccur.

The first thing that can be seen of the apparition is the headlight of the locomotive penetrating the fog. As the headlight gets closer, the many lights of the passenger car windows show the length of the train. As the misty locomotive reaches the crossing the horse and buggy suddenly appear; debris flies in every direction.

Years ago when young people wanted some chilling excitement, they would gather at the crossing on a suitable night and witness the spectacle. They say that when the watchers witnessed the ghostly scene, they were quite upset. With some viewers, their imagination was so strong that they thought that they could hear the crash and the screams of the horses and men.

Since the passing of Earl Day, who lived at the end of Wangum Road within easy view of the crossing, no one has kept a record of the phenomena. When he saw that the atmospheric conditions were going to be right, he would call interested persons to go to the crossing to make observations.

Since 1905 the stories of the ghost train have spread far and wide. Of course, there are non-believers, or so they say. It is interesting that they will not use the crossing when the sighting conditions are right but will go way out of their way to use another crossing.

# *The Pond with the Tropical Monsters*

Hiram Crossman and his tropical monsters have long been forgotten, but the pond which bears his name will always be a landmark. One of those many glacial kettle holes of the region, this one is located at the intersection of Fisher and Benson Roads. There are many in the area including those found in Mendon Ponds and Powder Mills Parks; some have water and others are without. Crossman's Pond has always had an air of mystery and speculation and was held in fear by older residents. It is known as a bone quarry because of lost cows and horses that went in and never came out. Only a stranger would swim in it.

Hiram Crossman's farmhouse overlooks the pond from Fisher Road. The sand sloped behind the house once contained fine peach and apple orchards, while the far reaches of the farm were for raising field crops. With a better than average income, and for health reasons, the Crossmans were able to winter in the tropics. The winter travels took the husband and wife to the West Indies and South America. A trip to the Galapagos Islands, off the coast west of Ecuador, impressed Mr. Crossman very much, for here he saw giant sea turtles and prehistoric-like giant lizards. He became obsessed with these monsters and arranged to have some of them brought back to Fishers, during the late 1870s.

The shallows of the pond grew an abundance of algae and insects, supposedly natural foods for the giant lizards and other creatures. The place teemed with all kinds of fish and edible weeds.

Hummocks and fallen trees made the pond an ideal habitat in the summer. Hiram liked his zoo, but others avoided it because of the large snakes and other frightful creatures. Heated rooms in the cellar were used in the bad weather.

Neither my parents nor anyone else could ever tell me what happened to the tropical reptiles. Some people think that in his old age he just left them in the pond to die. Through the succeeding years the pond has contained many large and small turtles. In 1942, a big turtle was pulled out of the pond which measured nearly four feet across its back.

About the year 1886 one of Hiram Crossman's snakes was blamed for a neighbor's death. Ben Smart lived at the place later known as the Battam's Farm, now subdivided. In the rear of the property now owned by Dr. Glenn Piper, Ben Smart had cleared a roadway from Fisher Road through to Log Cabin Road. A huge brush pile had been left to dry. No one was around on the day he burned it. When he did not return that night a search was made and he was found burned to death. In the ashes around him was the burned skeleton of a large snake the size of one of those owned by Hiram Crossman. The authorities reasoned that when the brush fire started to burn, a scorched snake came out and wrapped itself around Ben Smart, causing him to fall into the fire. Large snakes are common in caves and the warm woods under pine and hemlock roots giving the area the name of Snake Hollow.

# *The Great Wagon Sales*

The great wagon sale days were the next thing to a county fair. It was very similar to the present day farm machinery extravaganzas, but on a much smaller scale.

About every five years from 1885 until 1910, several companies brought their vehicles to Fishers to sell to buyers from the four-county area. The setting was made as festive as possible and covered all available space from the railroad station out into the surrounding fields. Surplus Civil War tents were used for shelters, sales shops, and serving food. The Valentown Band provided music from the bandstand. Those gala days gave the local families the opportunity to sell anything that they considered surplus, such as maple syrup, cheese, baked goods, quilts and other handwork and canned goods.

The idea was started by the Studebaker Brothers Manufacturing Company of South Bend, Indiana. Fishers was selected for the sale because it was in the center of a heavy potato producing area, which used a better grade of farm wagons. They sent a trainload of wagons to be assembled upon arrival, as did others with farm machinery to be exhibited. All types of riding vehicles and carriages were brought in and sold. Residents of Rochester's posh East Avenue came out on the train to buy fancy coaches and sports carriages. My father bought a fancy surrey-with-the-fringe-on-top.

Dealers and traders in horses did a brisk business. It was "buyer beware" when dealing in horses. One had to know how to pick a good horse vs. one that was doctored up to look good.

On the day of the last show, Charles Wiley shod a local horse in his blacksmith shop. The next day the horse hobbled back to the blacksmith shop by itself. Mr. Wiley recognized the horse as one that he had worked on the day before. He discovered that a nail had been driven into a tender spot on its hoof—and the horse came back to get relief!

In the evenings after the sales, local fiddlers and musicians provided the music for a street dance or a sing-along. Some tried out their own compositions. One who never made the big time was Al Barg. He liked to sing this one:

Old Billy Lord From Fishers town, I suppose you all do know, damndest old grey horse you ever did see go. Sometimes he drives to Fishers town and sometimes to the mill. But before he gets back he stops at the Mendon still.

Billy Lord's reply to Al Barg went this way:

How do you feel, Al? I am a little bit better than I have been, but not as good as I was. Well, goodbye, Al. When you come up, come down.

# The World's Largest Radio Set

Henry Phillips on Phillips Road owned the largest and the only radio set of its kind in the world. It was as big as an old fashioned hot air furnace. It WAS the hot air furnace located in his cellar. There were no knobs for adjusting the sound or station control. By just opening the furnace door, the radio program came out loud and clear. The Phillips house was at the foot of the hill on which the WHAM radio statin transmitter was located.

For those people who were energy-conscious this radio set/stove was very exciting as it did not require electric batteries nor any electric wiring which might go wrong. The Phillips family

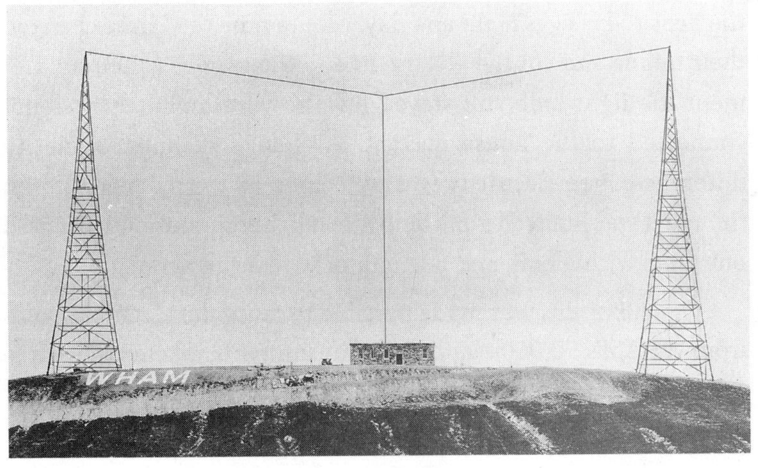


WHAM's first transmitter in 1927.

was kept busy in those early days of radio entertaining their neighbors and allowing in a whole procession of electrical engineers who were trying to solve the mystery of how a furnace could also be a radio set. Henry's oversize radio set even made Ripley's *Believe It Or Not.*

Henry Phillips was not the only person around Fishers with free radio privileges. Most everyone could listen to a radio program by just putting the telephone receiver to their ear. This was all very enjoyable until a few of the neighbors began getting enormous telephone bills for toll calls actually lasting only three or four minutes. Mrs. Lillian Leahy got a bill for $55.00 for a three-minute toll call to Rochester; the operator claimed that she could continuously hear voices and thought that Mrs. Leahy was still talking. That killed our instant radio service, because the telephone and radio engineers did something which took away those convenient programs.

There was nothing dull about life around Fishers. The Cline brothers had an electric light in their chicken coop to coax the hens to lay eggs night and day. After a time the Clines changed their minds and cut the electric line to the coop. To their amazement the light bulb still stayed lit. The wire definitely was not connected to the house current. A change of bulbs made no difference. Free electricity was welcomed by the neighbors, even though it was limited to one bulb. We neighborhood youths lighted our tents with a bulb and a length of wire as an aerial.

All of this was made possible because the electric current from WHAM's 50,000–watt radio transmitter blanketed the whole Fishers community. While it lasted, it made an interesting interlude in country living.

# *Musicians*

When the Fishers fancifully-designed band wagons pulled by four white horses came down the street with the musicians playing martial music on militia muster day, all spectators stood at rapt attention.

These days were prescribed by the New York State Legislature for military training and so were made into festive occasions. The units in various communities trained ahead for these musters, which were held in larger villages. Every able-bodied man in the state was obliged to register for training. Regiments were organized for infantry, cavalry, and artillery with commissions given officers.

The Fishers company was a part of the 4th Regiment of the 39th Brigade established in 1824. William Woolston was Captain, Erastus Ford was Lieutenant, and Charles Fisher was the Sergeant.

The military balls held by the officers of the militia were gala events. The Fishers Military Band played at some of those balls. Moreover, this band set the pattern for future local musicians by training new recruits.

In the spring of 1861, when the Civil War had broken out, Samual Valentine had just finished the construction of several barns. In order to show his patriotism, he painted the buildings the color of the American flag. On the 4th of July, the whole community conducted a patriotic rally in order to show support for President Lincoln, at what was then called the "Union Barns."

The band drove up in their wagon. Speeches and a basket picnic lunch made the day. Several young men were so affected by the music and the speeches that they joined the army.

When Valentown Hall was built in 1879, the Fishers Military Band had become the Valentown Band and used the ballroom for practice and concerts. A school of music was established on the second floor for students in both band and orchestra music. William A. Williams was both music teacher and band leader. The Valentown Band graduated into the Victor Military Band but had a short existence, for the men were elderly.

Bands got a revival for ten years during the 1930s until the war, when William J. Melville of Rochester organized two bands, the South Perinton Band and the Turk Hill Band, with the same musicians playing in both. Every Thursday night a concert was given on the Fishers band stand. Albert Kossow headed the local musicians.

Valentown Band, Fishers, New York.

For four Saturdays during the month of July, 1937, I presented large pageants in three counties to dramatize the invasion of the French army against the Seneca Indians 250 years before. Band Director Melville composed a musical suite of eight pieces depicting the original important event. Those people who attended the Fishers concerts will long remember the whistling solos by Edith Allen accompanied by the band. She was a very popular and talented musician before her untimely death.

The last band here, the Fishers Drum and Bugle Corps, was organized for youth and directed by Fred Burroughs during the 1950s.

In his rhyming memoirs, Levi Valentine wrote in part about his life in his parents' log cabin in the 1840s:

When the neighbors and friends met together for an apple paring bee, they sat talking and chatting; everybody was filled with glee. When the apples were pared, cored and strung, then came the eats, pie, fried cakes, sweet cider, popcorn and cheese. Then for the games and music, all were happy and pleased. I remember Saul Richardson as he sat on the lumber pile. In the south room playing his violin while the rest of the party were tripping lightly over the floor.

In August of 1940, Elizabeth Ford Shilling from Fairport, who lived here in her youth, wrote me:

I have been told that you have bought Valentown Hall. If it is true please do not spoil its good old name. When it was finished (1879) we had a party. Mr. And Mrs. G. S. Wood at the head of the first Quadrille, his eldest son, Charles J. Wood, danced at the foot of the set. The second son, Allie, with his sister, Verna, at one side. The younger son, Orson B. Wood, and Libbie Ford helped to fill out the set. There were other sets dancing at the same time. The music was furnished by George W. Hill from Main Street, Fishers, who certainly loved to play first violin and refused any pay but a box of cigars. Alonzo Benson of Benson Road played second violin. One or the other called the figure and was assisted by Cullen Rose, who played a horn. After that a club was organized; the Ford boys, the Woods, Adams and George Kreag and many others. Often an orchestra was hired from Rochester who came by train to Fishers. Oh, yes, we certainly had merry times.

Before the second floor of the Proseus Store next to the station was made into an apartment in 1900, it was a popular dance hall. The floor over Jones' Store and Wiley's Blacksmith Shop were also used for community activities such as dancing and church services. Before the Civil War, Quaker services were held over the blacksmith shop.

To have danced at Valentown Hall gave you special distinction. To listen to the descendants of those people who once danced here, it must have been a privilege to have done so. The descendants of the musicians who once played here also make much of that fact. Another great honor, it seems, was to have met your mate at Valentown. My father and mother met here in a play in 1905.

During the 1890s, for ultrasocial events F. V. Marthage's Harp Orchestra was hired, and had a run of about twenty years. The Fagan family orchestra, also from Rochester, came here. I remembered them as the elite orchestra during World War I when they played for the military balls presented by the Fishers Home Defense Reserve Company F.

From left: Jack "Fiddler" Barry,
Robert Barry (his grandson), and Ernest Barry.

John "Fiddler" Barry of Fowler Street and his son, Ernest, with Tom Hunt calling, provided the old time folk music during the first twenty years of the new century. The grandsons, Howard and Thomas Barry, continued the tradition in later years.

In January, 1861, Jeremiah Sullivan bought a log cabin

and lot from my great-grandfather on West Main. He had a son, John, who had an eye kicked out by a mule. They later sold the property and moved to Addison, New York. Jack later got home-sick and came back and worked as a farm hand. He talked so much about Addison that he was given the name of "Addison Jack." He was more often called "One-Eyed Jack," but not to his face. He owned an exceptionally fine violin and played at house parties. I liked to hear him play, for when he failed a note, he dubbed it in with a groaning sound.

For the economy-minded party promoters, Roscoe Griswold was the man. He was known as the one-man band and played many instruments at the same time. When Roscoe's house at the corner of Main Street and Log Cabin Road burned during the night, his dog saved his life.

Paul Nichols, a retired vaudeville entertainer, could play any musical instrument as well as imitate them in a musical composition or as an accompanist. Mark Hoskins played violin, with his wife at the piano, for dances at Valentown and at the Proseus Hall.

The Cline brothers, Irving, Charles and Grant, who lived on Phillips Road, gained much fame as musicians. They played in all area bands at some time or other. They had their own dance orchestra, with Edgar Lyons as the caller. Irving Cline was given the honor of New York State Champion Fiddler. He composed some of his own music and quadrilles. When competing orchestra leaders, such as D. K. Brownell, came into one of his dances, he would lay down his violin. He did not want any competitor to memorize his music. I saved five suitcases of his music from his estate.

Kingsley DeForest Brownell, a powerful Civil War veteran

and operator of the Fishers Mill, played the clarinet in the old Valentown Band. His son, DeForest K. Brownell, had his own dance orchestra for many years. He played first violin and Charles Smith played second violin; Mrs. Brownell played piano, and her son, James Snively, played bass violin. Wesley Smith played drums, and his uncle, Walter Smith, called the figures. Kingsley Brownell, the son of DeForest, carried on as a musician. The Brownell opening dance music was always a waltz, followed by Paul Jones, a circular dance as a mixer. Other dances were Perry Queen, Money Musk, Brooks Waltz, Quadrille, Lancers, Plain Quadrille, etc. Old King Brownell was opposed to his son's dance orchestra. He often said that his son, D. K., wasn't worth a damn. All he could do was to fiddle and he couldn't even dress a millstone, although his was a very popular orchestra.

It was a fad to hold dances and dinners in the large area homes during the 1930s. Music for these were provided by Kingsley Brownell, Jr., on the banjo, Howard Barry and Kermit Kossow with trumpets and Albert Kossow with the accordion; Tom Hunt was the caller.

Normally, all of the social parties through the years were wonderful friendly events, except for one. The dance held at Jones' Hall on February 27, 1915, was billed as something special. What happened shocked the whole community.

Twenty-two year old Howard Emory of Lower Fishers Road, in a jealous rage, shot his 17 year-old girlfriend, Irene Davis, who had refused to marry him. At 2:30 a.m. after the dance, thinking her dead, he turned his Colt .44 caliber army pistol on himself and died instantly. Howard did not know that Irene was dancing with her cousin during the evening. She was the niece of Mrs. George Jones and was the weekend guest.

I remember the event well. A number of the guests met at our house and left their horses in our barn. Howard Emory left his motorcycle at our house, and when my father took his coat to hang it on the rack, the pistol fell out on the floor. Little did we know how he planned to use it. Irene used to visit in Fishers for several years as she grew up.

# *The Runaway Slave*

Bedtime stories told to children are seldom forgotten. Among the many stories told to me and my brothers and sisters was one about the secret hiding place off one of our upstairs bedrooms in the Fisher homestead. Before the Civil War it was used as a hideout for runaway slaves escaping to Canada via the "Underground Railroad." Those escaping were hidden in loads of hay or boxes and were taken from one secret place to another.

One story is well remembered because we still have the razor given in gratitude to my great-grandfather Charles Fisher and also the iron handcuff removed from the slave's wrist. This man had been captured in Rochester and was being escorted in accordance with the law, by Sheriff Phineas Kent, to the Canandaigua Jail where his southern owner was to pick him up.

It was a cloudy night in October, 1847, when train #3 of the Rochester and Auburn Railroad left Rochester at 7:30 p.m. The train was loaded with passengers, but they were calm about the runaway slave in their midst. When the train reached Fishers, a plan to free the slave was carried out. As passengers alighted, the train was rushed from all sides by several dozen men and boys with their faces smudged black with burnt cork, creating a scene of great confusion. The engineer and train crew were held up, as planned. There was so much yelling and milling about that it was not possible to tell the slave was being helped to escape.

When the train was allowed to leave and Sheriff Kent realized the escape, many wagons and carriages loaded with black-faced people dashed in all directions. The Sheriff had to go on to Canandaigua empty handed. The young black was in a carriage which stopped at the Fisher homestead. He was then hidden in the secret room above the kitchen until danger of his recapture was past.

# Mud Pies Helped Build
# the Panama Canal

Down on the creek behind 342 Fisher Road is where little John G. Sullivan played beside a flowing spring. There was nothing unusual about this except that some lessons were learned by playing in the mud and studying the flow of water from one level to another. This same study was used on one of the world's greatest engineering feats. Little John was intrigued by the locks on the nearby Erie Canal and so designed some miniature locks on his creekside playground.

In 1882 a French company had started excavations for a sea level canal at Panama but soon went bankrupt. The United States bought out the French in May, 1904, and John G. Sullivan, who was by 1905 a Cornell graduate engineer, was sent to Panama to draw up plans to connect the Pacific and Atlantic oceans by a canal.

Chief Engineer John F. Stevens was stationed in Washington in order to keep Congress informed so they would supply the money. Sullivan was acting Chief Engineer on the project and sent his reports back to Washington. Congress was convinced by Stevens that a sea level canal would be impossible. One of the first obstacles to a sea level route was the 12–foot high Pacific tide, which would cause severe landslides along the canal banks. Sullivan found that the mountainous Atlantic-Pacific divide on the south side of Panama called for the building of a lock level canal.

John G. Sullivan's boyhood play back in Fishers came to

Private coach of John Sullivan on the Fishers Siding.
Sullivan was the famed engineer for building the
Panama Canal and the Canadian railroads.

mind when he found the Chagres River flowed from the eastern mountains into the lower Atlantic Ocean. He could duplicate his childhood canal locks by building a controlled lock system, which would be cheaper and faster to accomplish. He removed enormous amounts of volcanic silt by cutting through the Culebra and Obispo Ridges. When this was done, the water from the Chagres River could be used to raise boats over the continental divide. Using his mathematical and engineering expertise, he designed machines used in building the canal which made enormous savings on the cost of the canal.

In 1915 Sullivan began three years as Chief Engineer of the Canadian Pacific Railway, and then went into other work during the war. I remember the times when his private coach was switched to the siding next to Fowler's store when he came home to visit his parents. To us boys he came back as a hero recognized by society as an engineering genius. I was always glad that I had the chance to visit with him and get some of his stories firsthand.

The list of all of his engineering accomplishments is impressive. He engineered the construction of many railroad tunnels in the United States and Canada. The Canadian Pacific Railroad wanted to name a tunnel at Kooteny Lake, in British Columbia, after him but he objected. In order to have their way, they reversed the spelling of his name and called it the Navillus Tunnel.

John G. Sullivan was born in 1863, the oldest son of Thomas and Honorah Sullivan, who settled in Fishers in 1855 after coming from Trelee, Ireland the year before. Thomas met his wife at Lodi in Seneca County. They had eleven children and each one distinguished himself in some way.

Michael became a prominent mining engineer and was a successful prospector in the Klondike gold rush of 1896.

Jeremiah taught school in the Wanghum Academy in 1890, and his sister Margaret was one of his students. He became a civil engineer for the Canadian Pacific Railway and served in the Canadian Army during World War I. King George personally awarded him a decoration for valor at Vimy Ridge. I will never forget "Jerry" for the imposing figure he was in his Canadian Major's uniform.

Thomas, also a Cornell graduate, became a successful lawyer in Buffalo.

Brother Patrick also went to Buffalo and was a special guard for President McKinley at the Pan-American Exposition the day he was mortally wounded by an assassin. Patrick, like his brothers, was a big powerful man and knocked down the killer,

Leon Czolgosz, and held him. In the melee Patrick was knocked unconscious with a 2x4 stick and a news reporter used the name of another person as the one who made the capture. Nevertheless, President Theodore Roosevelt recognized Patrick as the one making the capture and presented him with a gold- headed cane.

Katherine spent her life making a home for the family and was a very respected lady in Fishers.

James was a jolly and powerful man and operated their two farms. Just his presence as a bouncer at all Fishers dances scared those who might want to cause trouble. I saw "Jim" one day when he got off the train from Rochester. He said that three men tried to knife and rob him. He hit one of the men so hard with his fist that he died on the spot. The other two were knocked out and were taken to the hospital.

I remember their father, Thomas, very well. He had a witty Irish approach to everything the same as many others who immigrated during the Irish potato famine of the 1840s and 50s.

One of his remarks, while cutting wood with others was "give me room according to my strength." He was a very forthright person and very shrewdly avoided artful traps. I heard him say once, "no one was going to put him in Joe Pardy [jeopardy]." When his children were young, he attended school with them in Fishers.

He was known as "Big Tom" and one day some men were bragging about their strength at the Fishers Mill. He made a deal with Old King Brownell, the mill owner and a powerful man himself. Big Tom could have a 196–pound barrel of flour if he could carry it home without putting it down. It was a mile uphill from the mill to his house and several men went along to check. Tom walked into the kitchen with the barrel on his shoulders and called, "Norie, look at the nice present the miller gave us."

Even though all of his relatives were over here, Big Tom got so homesick for Ireland that he had to go back for a visit. While driving through the Irish countryside, he saw a man holding a plow while his wife was trying to pull it. Tom got out of his buggy in a burst of indignation and beat up the man. He had expected Irish men to have more respect for women and thus never wanted to go back again.

# *Superlatives*

In the period around World War I, the trend seemed to be to think "big." There was a feeling of outdistancing the other fellow, by doing something bigger and better—in farming and everything else.

The bake sales to raise money for the various social clubs which met at Valentown Hall produced goods which were so unusual that they were mentioned in a number of diaries. Some pies were so "big" that they were purchased for banquets in nearby towns. Mrs. John McCarthy made a fried cake so "big" that it had to be cooked in a washtub. Mrs. Emma Ford on Fisher Road made tasty cruller-like pastry in "big" quantities for "big" parties. They were called "MineEmma's" because Fred Ford was proud to say that they were made by "mine Emma."

"Doc" Frank Woolston, a veterinarian, sold "huge" automobiles with enormous bodies and wide expanses of glass, making the passenger cars look like store showcases. Ambrose Ford sold the "greatest" number of Ford cars. "Doc" also had a Case gas-driven tractor with a "huge" single drive wheel, the "largest" and most cumbersome piece of machinery which could be imagined. (I always kept my distance for fear that it would tip over on me.) In order to house all of his animals, hay, and veterinary equipment, he had Charles Wiley build him the "biggest" barn in the area.

Noah Baker had built the "biggest" lumber wagon ever seen in these parts for hauling potatoes to the Fishers station. He also had built the "highest" barn on the "highest" hill in these parts, a thousand feet above sea level. Roy Battams and King Brownell had the "biggest" log wagons with the "highest" wheels. Clara Fisher had the "biggest" flower garden. Several had the "largest" telephones, that is, built like a grandfather's clock case. Mrs. Joseph Barnes had the "largest" cat. One person complained of having the "largest" debt.

My grandfather's orchard had trees which produced the "biggest" red apples, the Wolf River, but it was not a tasty apple.

Bill Sullivan raised the "biggest" Hubbard squash on his muckland off Log Cabin Road. It was the "biggest" job to load them on his wagon for exhibition at the county fair where he took honors. For his extra "big" squash, he fed them sour milk and buttermilk by laying a vine into the milk pan. This gave the squash more nourishment, which made for enormous growth. This same technique was used for our Wolf River apple tree, but we poured the milk at the base of the trees.

A hired man for A. G. Aldridge Seed Potato Company of Fishers tried out the sour milk process on a hill of potatoes on the Aldridge farm on Valentown Road. He removed all potatoes from the vine except one. The milk pan was kept full. The hired man had to keep piling the soil higher and higher in order to keep the potato covered. When harvest time came, the tuber had grown to the size of a large watermelon. At the county fair it was hailed as the world's "largest" potato. When the Aldridge warehouse was sold, I went to save the photograph of the potato, but it had just been burned.

When people gathered in groups around town, quite often they got to talking about places where they had been or would see who could tell the "biggest" story. King Brownell, the village miller, usually could out-tell the best of them, and I am sorry that I can't remember his choicest. One he told about was when he was in the Civil War. The captain wanted volunteers to get a cook stove across the Potomac River. King agreed to do the job because he considered himself a good swimmer. The stove was placed upon his back, and he soon delivered it to the opposite shore.

He often told about a strange experience while lumbering nearby. As he leaned against a hollow tree, considering where he should drop it, he felt the tree contracting and expanding in a somewhat even rhythm. Never having experienced anything like this before, he investigated. He found that the hollow tree was packed full of live raccoons. In order for them to breath in such tight quarters, they all had to do so in unison. King didn't have the heart to cut down the tree.

My grandfather, William Fisher, got struck with what my neighbors claimed was the "biggest" bolt of lightning when he was standing under the old hickory tree back of the barn. His clothes and shoes were torn from his body, and his hoe handle was split into slivers. His body was quite burned, but after a time he regained consciousness and found that he suffered no other ill effects.

"Aunt" Kate McCarthy, in her old age, loved to fish with her long bamboo pole in the swimming hole back of the mill. She caught more trout than those who used fancy fishing gear. One day she had to call for help to land a fish that was so "big" that she couldn't get it out of the water. "Uncle" Johnny Haley hurried to her rescue, along with several others. On her hook they could see a speckled trout, but as they kept pulling it out there didn't seem to be any end. Longer and longer it went until there was about fifteen feet of it. What "Aunt" Kate had was an eel with the fish tail in its mouth, along with three other three-foot eels biting the tail of the one ahead. I am ashamed to say that I had thrown a dead woodchuck into the stream, which had brought a concentration of eels to feed upon the carcass.

"Maggie Murphy" potato pictured in
Sarah Murphy's potatoe seed catalog.

# When the Threat of Hell Scared the Hell Out of Victor

Like many communities on the frontier during the early half of the nineteenth century, Victor, New York had its share of ruffians, drunkards and blasphemers, although the situation was not as violent as it was in the Wild West. Many of the unpolished residents here were the ones who came to work on building the Erie Canal and the Auburn and Rochester Railroad. The more religious settlers were in sufficient numbers to support three churches: Presbyterian, Methodist and Universalist, for religion in western New York these were unsettling times.

In 1730 Jonathan Edwards set in motion the great religious upheaval in Massachusetts which was brought on to western New York. The text of one of Rev. Edwards' sermons at Northhampton, Massachusetts was "Sinners in the hands of an angry God" who, if they didn't repent and be saved would suffer eternal "Fire and Brimstone."

Joseph Smith from the Town of Manchester announced his "true" religion given him by angel visitations before 1830. Sixty members of the Mendon Baptist Church were baptized into the Mormon faith in Brigham Young's nearby millpond on a freezing April day.

In 1848, Spiritualism got its start in Hydesville, near Newark in Wayne County, when two little girls, Margaret and Katherine Fox, demonstrated their ability to communicate with the spirit of a peddler who had been murdered earlier in their house.

When the Fox family moved to Rochester, the peddler's spirit went with them.

Charles Fisher became interested in Spiritualism because of the recent deaths of his wife and two daughters. Seances were held in the Fisher homestead. Once Margaret Fox left her tortoise shell comb there, which is still preserved by this author along with the spirit writings and books. Many famous people became interested in Spiritualism, which swept the country and spread to Europe.

William Miller, who lived in Low Hampton, New York, near the Vermont border, was a serious student of the Bible. He assembled prophesies from the Old and New Testaments in a very convincing sequence to set the date of the second coming of Christ and the end of the world. He calculated the time as about 1843, and others later refined it to be October 22, 1844.

Miller and his friends felt it their duty to alert the public to the seriousness of his discovery. In 1831 at Dresden, New York near Lake Champlain, he made his first startling announcement. It grabbed the attention of all religious-minded people of the time. The great shower of meteorites in 1833 was taken as more proof of the end of the world.

The student followers of William Miller were known as Millerites and got a hearing in many churches. Rev. Zina J. Buck of the Victor Methodist Church invited a Millerite to speak. Then he objected to the message and expelled nearly half of his congregation who believed the message. They built their own church across the street at the foot of Piety Hill where the Victor "saved" were supposed to have climbed the hill wrapped in bed sheets to be ready to ascend to heaven at the appointed time.

Even those who had sinned or transgressed in minor ways

began to be frightened about being confined in an eternal fire. No longer did the drunken village bully ride his horse up and down the main street singing bawdy songs and cursing God. The bully was converted. The village saloons were closed and the immoral people became model citizens—at least until the crucial date.

The bells in the belfries of the three churches, tuned differently and rung in sequence each Sunday, seemed to sound to the residents the doctrine of that denomination. The Presbyterian bells rang out "Church Time, Church Time." The Methodist bells rang, "Repent, Repent." The Universalist bells followed with "No Hell, No Hell." The No Hell appealed to me when attending the Universalist Church before and during World War I. The same messages of these bells continued until the closing of the Universalist Church about 1924 and then the bell was sold to the Lima Presbyterian Church, when theirs was destroyed by lightning.

For 50 cents a Sunday I had a job at the Universalist Church pumping the air for the large pipe organ during the years 1918– 20. When the three bells stopped ringing, it was my time to start pumping air. The pump handle, which looked like a well pump handle, was located in a stuffy closet behind the organ. On a hot day there was very little oxygen and I often went to sleep. One song required a great deal of wind, more than I provided when I went to sleep. The organ stopped in the middle of the singing, much to my chagrin and the embarrassment of the organist.

At the time appointed for the end of the world to come, the followers of William Miller of Port Gibson, Town of Manchester, Ontario County, gathered in a barn owned by Hiram Edson and waited and waited until midnight. But no end of the world came, so they reacted like hundreds of other disappointed hopefuls. In Edson's words, "our fondest hopes and expectations were blasted and such a spirit of weeping came over us as I never expected before. It seemed that the loss of all earthly friends could have been no comparison. We wept and wept until the day dawned."

# *Cannonading the Thruway*

On the afternoon of July 10, 1965, traffic on the New York Thruway was stopped from both directions as cannon shells exploded on the median near the Fisher Road underpass. Clouds of dust were being thrown into the air in a path over the hill from the south. CB radios began calling for help and soon a State Police plane began circling the area.

Brian Donovan, a *Democrat & Chronicle* reporter who became suspicious of what might be happening, ran down the hill and called for the shooting to stop. The Seventh Annual Fishers Skirmish for the Northeast Region of the North-South Skirmish Association was in progress with about thirty regiments from New York and surrounding states.

The rifle and carbine matches by the infantry and cavalry had finished their targets at the base of a 200-foot-high hard, dry clay hill. A line of cannon began firing at their targets much to the pleasure of a large audience interested in the Civil War Centennial years.

What caused the problem was that the 1st New Jersey Volunteers had entered their high-powered original rifled Dahlgren cannons. Instead of penetrating the hard clay soil as expected, the shells instead cut a trench up and over the hill to fall again, a quarter of a mile further than expected, on the Thruway.

The host regiment, for two days and three nights each year, was the First New York Dragoons—the cavalry regiment from Fishers. The picturesque Civil War encampment was in the

The cannon that accidently blasted the
New York State Thruway with shot.

rear on the Fisher family hill. The Dragoons had camped at the target range the night before. Although outlawed now, the targets were sticks of dynamite. The Dragoon Skirmish Director, Roy McLean, the next morning called for the dynamite and was told that he had slept on it all night; he immediately vomited because he was so shocked. The Dragoon demolition expert had forgotten where he had hidden the explosives. Tension among the skirmishers was so strong that the annual military costume ball at the Fishers Fire Hall was a complete failure.

The skirmish was held at a new location because of the thruway trouble the year before. There the targets were at the base of a high railroad embankment, and the shooting was parallel to the Thruway. Again, the cannons were the undoing of the event.

Several poor cannoneers missed their mark, and the shells ripped down the telegraph lines from Rochester to New York, Philadelphia and Washington.

Now each year the annual Fishers Skirmish is held at a range east of Palmyra timed to be a part of the Palmyra Canal Days celebration.

This famous Western New York cavalry regiment had been re-activated in October, 1959 by this writer, and no other such problems have occurred in all of the years since. Assisting in the formation were two others who also had ancestors in the regiment, William Welch and Alexander Van. Retirees from the New York 121st Cavalry, which had mechanized, joined us with their horses. The outfit has been a huge success and has been called on for all types of functions. The roster has included over 150 men from five counties and is now dismounted. The First New York Dragoons rate high in the NSSA as cap and ball shooters and travel to the range twice a year in Winchester, Virginia. The Dragoon headquarters is at the Valentown Museum.

# Local Quotes

Allen kept having so many babies that Dr. Alfred Mead lost his patience. He took Allen aside and said that the "Lord put us on this globe to populate the earth, but he didn't say that one man should do it all."

The names of three neighbors on Boughton Hill south of Victor village years ago provided much entertainment for those who liked unusual quips: "I. Ketchum, U. Killam, and I. Eadum."

Miller "King" Brownell admonished us boys with "One boy is a boy, two boys are a half a boy, and three boys are no boy at all, and so get out."

"Dirty face Nick" Romonoff peddled his own all purpose herb meat tenderizer shortly after World War I. He had an open buggy pulled by an old horse. He lived in a run down house near the end of West Main Street, Fishers. Not having a barn, he kept the horse in his kitchen. His pet chickens roosted on his bed post—hence his name of "Dirty face Nick."

Morris Leahy fresh from Ireland in the 1880s made remarks his neighbors liked to repeat. When Morris and Jack "Fiddler" Barry were having an argument, Jack called Morris a number of hard names. Morris said, "Sure and how can I be all of them names you are calling me? Sure and it's very easy to fool a blind horse. You put in a little straw in the manger and tell him its hay and he believes it. Sure and you expect me to be a fool like the horse to believe what you call me."

# *Jacqua and Soeka Gahgwa*

Jacqua and Soeka Gahgwa were friends. They were never together in the daytime but only at night. Often Jacqua would communicate in a loud manner sometimes to the distress of those nearby. Soeka Gahgwa was never known to answer, but Jacqua didn't mind, for he knew that Soeka Gahgwa couldn't answer for he was millions of miles out in space. Today we call Soeka Gahgwa the moon.

This Seneca Indian story about the two has lasted for more than 300 years. Jacqua was a very unusual dog and lived in the large Seneca Indian town of Ganondagan. This remarkable dog had abilities of mind, hearing, smell and action far beyond any ordinary animal. It knew the thoughts of any person whether it be good or bad and acted accordingly.

Jacqua was a self-appointed sentry looking out for the best interest of the people of this hill-top town. If there were people of ill intent coming towards Ganondagan from miles away, Jacqua knew it. He had a way of warning the war chiefs who prepared for the proper defense. Jacqua patrolled the trails north, south, east and west with great satisfaction to the Chief's Council. However, one time when the chiefs were all away Jacqua had no one to warn when danger approached.

The Iroquois tribe of Huron looked down upon their Seneca cousins south of Lake Ontario and created a state of war. A single Huron chopped his way into a bark long house during the night. Despite the warnings of Jacqua no one took heed until it was too late. Ever after all persons listened to Jacqua with special attention. He served a full dog's life to be memorialized in history and legend.

Generations of story-tellers kept alive this and other tales about Jacqua down to a blind Tonawanda Seneca Indian by the name of Simeon Skye who was by trade a piano tuner. Over 70 years ago he kept the Valentown Hall ballroom piano in tune. When his vision was not so blurred, he was often taken to his ancestral home on Boughton Hill south of Victor, New York, now Ganondagan State Historic Site.

# The Locomotive Bobsled

The mountainous hills around Honeoye Lake of the Finger Lakes were cleared of virgin timber about the year 1906. Aiding in this task for getting the logs off the mountain top, the Klondike Lumber Company built a railroad from the lake shore up the treacherous gorge of Briggs' Gully to Gulick Swamp the haven of rattlesnakes. This gully is on the southeast end of the lake.

For the safety of the crew in the cramped quarters of the gorge the locomotive was built with a verticle boiler. The photograph shows a view of the locomotive with the crew with the log train. The first person on the left is Edward Olmstead, late of Victor. The second is William Myers, and on the right is Bert Clark. In the cab of the locomotive is the engineer William Skelton.

Coming down grade with a load of logs made the train wheels screech on the sharp curves. One day the boss's son could not stand the noise any longer, and so he greased the rails, without warning the train crew.

Engineer Skelton had ventured to take on a heavier load. As he was slowly going down grade towards the dreaded waterfalls curve, the train suddenly shot forward like a racing bobsled out of control. Putting on the brakes only made the train go faster. With good presence of mind the engineer hooked the stoking rod on the whistle cord to let the workers on the lake know that the train was out of control and coming at them. The train crew did not dare to jump but rode the train out into the lake without anyone getting hurt.

This event was talked about as long as the participants were alive. About eleven years after the train plunged into the lake, the boys from Fishers were taken on an annual weeks's vacation at the lake. It was always an event to go up the gully to see the final wreck of the log train with the tangled tracks wedged among the rocks of this exciting gorge.

# *Fire Fighting Hazards*

Pulling a two-wheeled chemical fire-fighting cart is as dangerous as any fire-fighting work. This I found out when I helped pull the cart for the year-old Fishers Chemical Fire Department to its first fire in 1921.

Hobos had set fire to a nearby barn. Everybody became a fireman. Men, women and children all pulled on the cart handle or on the long extended rope. It was a sight to see. An overabundance of cart pullers caused legs to get tangled and be run over like the ancient Juggernaut of India. I was felled in the melee and the high cartwheel barely missed my body.

Soon afterward Charles Wiley mounted the cart equipment on a second hand Model T Ford Chassis and made the truck look somewhat professional. In his blacksmith shop he forged parts to support a gong, steps to stand on and long bars to hold onto. Extra firemen added too much weight so they had to drive themselves.

I can still see Charles Wiley on the way to a fire standing on the running board continuously going through the motions of pulling the safety pin on the chemical tank to turn the brass wheel to rock the tank to mix the acid with the soda. The reason for practicing was so he would not fumble in getting water pressure when he arrived at the fire.

Never having had any fire training lessons, the men reacted strangely when the firebell rang. Once a man jumped onto the truck and before anyone else could get on, drove madly in the opposite direction. He hadn't waited to find out where the fire was.

Another man drove the truck off with the long hose dragging. Cars following drove onto the hose, causing it to stretch. Then when they got off, the hose snapped back like a rubber band and hit the rear end of the truck. Fortunately, no one was riding there.

The fire in a still during prohibition days was equal to a Laurel and Hardy comedy film when everybody began drinking the "Valley Dew" before the fire consumed it.

One stormy night a reckless driver was at the wheel. I was hanging on the side pulling the gong cord when I noticed that we were going to crash into an embankment at the end of Willis Hill Road at Dryer. Somehow I was able to turn off the ignition switch and avoid a catastrophe.

The roads long ago were often so full of ruts that firemen were sometimes bounced off the truck.

One bright spring noon a call came for a barn fire on the Elmer Woolston farm, now known as the Burroughs Audubon Nature Club. A driver and I took off as fast as the Model T truck could go. Up Fisher Road we went and down the long Railroad Mills Road. Then the brakes failed. Across the lawn we raced, just missing the burning barn. We jumped off before the truck plunged into Irondequoit Creek. I got the extension ladder up to the barn roof and sprayed the shingles with soda acid water while the man with the fire hose worked the interior. When my back began to feel warm I found that my pants were burning off. We lost the barn but saved the house.

Jack Woolston's barn exploded from overheated wet hay. My brother Francis, who was working for Jack, was last seen going into the barn. Our chemical tank charge sprayed and sprayed trying to find him, but to no avail. Under complete anxiety, a group of us were standing in the house kitchen, now office of Ted Collins Tree and Landscape Co., when a Victor fireman rushed in swinging an axe. He yelled out, "Where is your cistern?" Jack said it was underneath the floor. So the fireman began wildly chopping a hole in the inlaid floor. It was quite a job to subdue the fireman who was noted for his axe work. About that time my brother Francis drove up, returning from an errand. His safe appearance was a great relief to everyone.

After thirteen years, the member financed fire company stopped supporting it and the company faded away. In 1940 I set in motion a tax financed Fire District. Today it is one of the very finest and best equipped fire departments in Ontario County. It has two fine fire houses. But the fires fought in the Model T days with untrained firemen are something never to be forgotten.

# Ancestors
## Not a Social Disease

About the year 1900 a local boy by the name of Earl Pimm went beserk among his chums. One of his friends told him that he had a bad case of ancestors. Others chimed in and assured him that he certainly did. Thinking that ancestors was a social disease and that they were making fun of him, he began beating up his friends one by one.

If Earl had not been so hasty and let some one explain what ancestors really were, he might have been impressed.

Earl would have learned that his ancestors were his parents, grandparents, great-grandparents, and so on, doubling each generation back.

Like everyone else, he had eight great-grandparents. In ten generations it gets to be 1,024 ancestors. In fourteen generations the number would be 16,384 grandfathers and grandmothers. In forty generations the number of ancestors would be approximately two and two tenths trillion people.

# *The Author*

In 1940 J. Sheldon Fisher and his wife Lillian purchased Valentown Hall and established the Valentown Museum to house his collection that is as diverse as his interests. Iroquoiria, Military, Scientific, Folk Lore, Genealogical—all attrract the curiosity and investigation of the man "Hiawasees," the name given him by the Seneca Indians in 1964 at the time of his adoption by the Heron clan. It means "the eagle who gathers news and history" and it is an appropriate handle for Fisher who has spent most of his life gathering, chronicling, and preserving the history of western New York.

Professionally, he helped build the renown archaeological collection of the Rochester Museum and Science Center and became the first County Historian in Ontario County. Always active as a volunteer in community organizations, he was a founder of the Rochester Genealogical Society and the Fishers' Fire Department as well as reconstituting a Civil War cavalry regiment, the First New York Dragoons.

Shortly before his 80th birthday, in the summer of 1987, he was honored as a primary influence in the 42–year campaign that led to the dedication of Ganondagan, the first New York State Historic Site devoted to Natavie American culture.

*The Fish Horn Alarm* is his second publication of folk tales.